Lustleigh
A Dartmoor Village in focus

Published by The Lustleigh Society

Researched and written by Chris Wilson
Image research and project co-ordination by Karen Stevenson
Editorial support by Peter F. Mason

Copyright

The majority of the images in this book are held by the Lustleigh Community Archive and are therefore treated as being gifted to the archives to be preserved and used as is felt appropriate. Some images have been reproduced under licence to the copyright holders and are acknowledged accordingly.

For the remainder, every effort has been made to trace the copyright holders and obtain permission to reproduce this material. We are happy to correct any errors or omissions relating to copyright of an image or the rights holder in future editions.

Image Quality

Some of the images in this book have been reproduced from old or very poor-quality originals. Some were badly creased and damaged and have been skilfully digitally restored by Barbara Jaggs. You may find that some of the reproductions are lacking in clarity, however it was felt that the subject matter and importance of these images to the story of the village, justified including them here.

We often rely on the donor to provide information about the photographs they lodge with the archives with regard to people and places. Every effort has been made to publish the correct information about the image and names of any people featured therein. As above, we are happy to make any corrections as necessary in future editions.

Designed by Touchwood Design
Printed by Short Run Press

www.lustleigh-society.org.uk
ISBN:978-0-9957122-2-5

Front cover photograph by Rod Latham
Rear cover - Clockwise from top left: Village from top of Mill Lane (tinted postcard, Andrew Beer, date unknown); Beating the Bounds, standing at what was then the old boundary with Bovey Tracey (date unknown); View of Lustleigh, 1957; Haymaking at Kelly Farm showing Norah Wright holding the baby and Eric Bunclarke with the cider jar (date unknown, photo courtesy Courtney Wright).

Contents

Dedication

This book is dedicated to Jan Rowe (1938 – 2016)

The Lustleigh Society was started by a small group of enthusiasts in 1978. Over the years they amassed a large amount of data which was originally stored in their respective houses. A decision was made to relocate this material in the Reading Room of the Church House. Jan was appointed the Archivist. Over the years she curated, organised, indexed and collected material to add to the ever-growing collection. When the Archive relocated to The Old Vestry it was Jan who, every Monday afternoon, opened the archive room and manned it. Over the years she recruited various helpers and the archives blossomed under their care.

Jan was passionate about history and also about Lustleigh. When the decision was made to relocate the collection into an archive standard environment and computerise the catalogue, Jan handed the reins over to me. However, she continued to volunteer and take on special projects until ill health prevented her from doing so.

Now, our archive is regarded by many as one of the best on Dartmoor and is run with a team of some twenty curators and volunteers all of whom live in Lustleigh.

The Lustleigh Community Archive stands as testament to the people of Lustleigh, because over the course of the last forty years they have donated the majority of the data, kept it running on a weekly basis, offered freely their time, effort and expertise and organised and run numerous special research projects and events.

But largely, it is down to Jan who started it all….

Karen Stevenson, Archivist

Foreword

Lustleigh is a village and parish with centuries of history behind it. It gets few, if any, mentions in the history books but it has a story to tell – the story of the people who have lived in the area since prehistory, the work they did, the marks they left on the landscape, their buildings, customs and celebrations. To quote the words of Rowland Parker in his social history of Britain, *The Common Stream*, this is a story "of the ordinary men and women who in their countless thousands have trudged through life and then departed from it, leaving little visible trace. That little, multiplied a million-fold, constitutes a large slice of what we call our national heritage."

The Lustleigh Society founded in 1978, records, researches and preserves this history. The Lustleigh Community Archive holds parish records, maps including the 1837 Tithe Map, Parish Magazines dating from 1888, minutes of village organisations, press-cuttings, paintings, books, oral history recordings and many other documents of historic interest. It also possesses over 3,500 photographs and postcards of the parish and village life.

In 2001 the Society published *The Book of Lustleigh* which chronicled the history of the village and celebrated its residents at the Millennium. The book is now out of print and with a wealth of new material available the Society believes that the time has come to publish this book.

Lustleigh, a Dartmoor Village in focus is being published to mark the fortieth anniversary of the Society. Thanks are due to Karen Stevenson and Chris Wilson for bringing it to fruition. Numerous people have contributed to it, through loans and gifts to the Archive and through their research over the years. I would particularly pay tribute to those who wrote articles for The Book of Lustleigh and to Jan Rowe whose in-depth research for the permanent exhibition about the history of the village has formed the basis for this project.

We would also like to thank the Lustleigh Show Committee and Margaret Bowen, the Society's President, who have provided sponsorship.

Peter F. Mason, Chairman, The Lustleigh Society

Introduction

Lustleigh is a small scattered village in a romantic dell, deep in the valley of the Wrey Brook, nestled in a strikingly verdant landscape which, although once extensively farmed, is characterised by extensive areas of woodland. Opening to the valley of the Bovey River, it has been described as 'the most charmingly situated village in Devon'[1].

Lustleigh is a parish and a village, about one mile west of the main Bovey Tracey to Moretonhampstead road, with a disused station (now a private residence) on the old Great Western railway. It is about ten miles north west from Newton Abbot, four miles south east from Moretonhampstead and 192 miles from London. Lustleigh sits within Dartmoor National Park, the district council boundaries of Teignbridge and the parliamentary district of Central Devon.

The village is centred around the parish church of St. John the Baptist, occupying a site which is thought to have been an early Christian burial ground (prior to 550AD). Today, comprising some 3,333 acres, the parish boundaries have changed many times over the centuries, most recently in 1957 with the inclusion of the ancient manor of Wreyland. Also within its limits are the hamlets of Brookfield, Hammerslake, Pethybridge and Sanduck.

Lustleigh Cleave is a picturesque ravine of granite rocks of considerable extent running almost parallel with the valley in which the village stands. Hewn from a major fault-line, the Cleave's dramatic landscape has drawn comparisons with an Isle of Wight chine[2], Swiss-like scenery[3] and even a miniature canyon[4]; consequently, it has also long drawn thousands of tourists annually.

1. History

Geology

The parish of Lustleigh lies on the eastern boundary of the Dartmoor Granite which was squeezed up as a molten magma into the overlying sedimentary rocks of Carboniferous age some 280 million years ago. The sediments which covered the solidified granite have been eroded away through geologic time so that only those along the flanks of granite are now preserved: they have been severely altered by heat and are now described as quartzites and hornfels.

Through the north-east edge of the granite runs the great Lustleigh-Sticklepath Fault System which stretches from the Bristol Channel north of Lundy Island to the Bovey Basin and runs through our parish where there are two parallel tear, or strike-slip faults; San Andreas in California is another example of such a fault. At Lustleigh, one of these faults runs along the course of the Wrey Brook while the more important one follows the River Bovey Valley, including that adjacent to the fault scarp of Lustleigh Cleave.[5]

Fluids which permeated out from the granite gave rise to numerous metal and mineral deposits both in the granite itself and in the adjacent metasediments. There are records mentioning a disused tin mine near Peck on the north-western fringes of the parish while mines for micaceous haematite, including Kelly and Pepperdon, are to be seen just outside the parish boundary.

Another characteristic of the granite at Lustleigh is the beautiful large crystals of feldspar which appear to float in the finer grained matrix: this handsome rock was quarried at Haytor and used for the old London Bridge and the British Museum.

© Devon County Council, F.M. Griffith 22 December 1986

Hunter's Tor Iron Age Hill Fort, Lustleigh Cleave.

Early history

As is common across the whole of Dartmoor there are Bronze Age Hut Circles on Lustleigh Cleave and the Iron Age Hill Fort on Hunter's Tor is one of several such forts on the fringes of Dartmoor.

Evidence of an early Christian settlement in Lustleigh is seen in the classic features of a circular enclosed graveyard. The inscribed 'Datuidoc's' stone, dated 550AD, now housed in the church, is further evidence of an early burial site.

Aerial view of the churchyard showing circular shape. The shape was slightly altered when the road was constructed.

There is no recorded evidence of the Roman era in Lustleigh. Pre-Conquest Lustleigh must have consisted of a small population living in scattered farmsteads and hamlets.

The earliest known recorded mention of Lustleigh occurs in 901 in the will of Alfred the Great, in which the manor, then known as Sutreworde (South of the Wood), was left to his youngest son. Under the same name, it appears in the Domesday Book, by which time the Manor comprised some 1200 acres, a large part of which was woodland. Pig breeding and raising sheep were the main occupations, and bee-keeping was also recorded - one of the few mentions of this in King William's 1086 'Great Survey'.

Lords of the Manor

In 1065, the Manor of Lustleigh was held by Ansgar and prior to that by one Walter. After a gap in the records, we then find a 13th century Lord of the Manor, Sir William de Widworthy; it is thought that the effigies in the north wall of Lustleigh Church of a knight and lady may be those of Sir William and his wife, Juliana, although there are competing theories including Sir William's son Sir Hugh and his wife and Sir Robert Dinham and Lady Emma Dinham, Sir Hugh's daughter.

Hugh de Widworthy inherited the manor from his father and in turn the title passed to his daughter, Emma Dinham, who with her husband Robert were Lord and Lady of the manor until 1291, but having had no children the manor passed to Emma's cousin William le Prous[6], of whom there is also an effigy in Lustleigh church.

On the death of Sir William le Prous in 1316, the manor passed to his daughter Emma, who was married to Roger de Moelis. It then passed to their daughter Alice de Moelis and her husband John Daumarle; then to their son, Sir John Daumarle and his wife Isabella; as they were childless, it then passed to Clarice, Sir John's sister, who was married to Richard Grenville. There is some uncertainty as to who succeeded them, as by rights it should have been Clarice's daughter and in turn her daughter, but historical evidence suggests that these women were tricked out of their rightful inheritance by the machinations of the sons of Isabella by her first marriage to John Tremayne.

In 1403 the manor was sold to Sir John Wadham, a noted judge, and it remained in the possession of the Wadham family for the next 200 years and six generations. However, the Wadhams appear never to have been resident in Lustleigh, their family seat being at Edge in the parish of Branscombe, East Devon. They acquired many estates and when the last male heir, Nicholas Wadham, died in 1609 he was one of the richest men in the kingdom; with his wife Dorothy, he founded Wadham College, Oxford.

The Tithe Map

In 1836 Parliament passed an Act by which every parish parson would receive annually a cash payment called the Tithe Rent replacing the old system of payment in kind. Detailed maps were made showing each dwelling, the boundaries of each field, and giving the field a number.

Schedules had to be drawn up concerning every farm and cottage, listing the fields by their number on the Tithe Map and stating the name of the owner, the occupier and of each field. Also recorded was the acreage and whether the field was arable, pasture, orchard etc. The amount of Tithe Rent to be paid annually was thereby assessed.

Lustleigh's Tithe Map and Schedules give us a complete historical picture of the parish as it was in

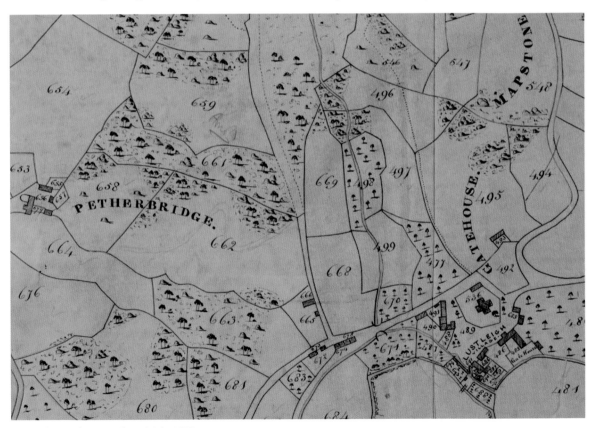

Extract from Tithe Map of Lustleigh, 1837.

the year 1837. The Lustleigh Society is fortunate to have an original map in its archive. We can see from this that the boundary of Lustleigh on the eastern side was the river Wrey, while on the opposite side was the manor of Wreyland, which until recently was in the parish of Bovey Tracey. Wreyland, referred to in records from the 14th century onwards, now consists of a group of thatched cottages forming a small hamlet.

Boundary changes (in 1957) finally brought Wreyland into the parish of Lustleigh. At the same time Kelly, Knowle and Brookfield came within the boundaries of Lustleigh. Kelly and Knowle were old established farm estates but Brookfield initially developed because of the need to house the workers at Kelly Mine in the late nineteenth century. During an earlier boundary change (1885) Pepperdon was transferred to Moretonhampstead while Sanduck passed from North Bovey to Lustleigh.

Historical artefacts found in the parish: Roman Brooch, Henry II (1154 –1189) silver coins showing obverse and reverse.

2. Railway

G.W. RY. STATION. LUSTLEIGH 12487

Postcard Chapman & Son

Before the railway came to Lustleigh, the community was closely linked to agriculture, the population consisting mostly of farmers, farm labourers and craftsmen who supported the farming life.

From the 1840s, following the rapid expansion of the railway system over the whole country, branch lines were seemingly opening everywhere and in the late 1850s a group of prominent local landowners decided that a company should be formed to construct a line from the South Devon main line at Newton Abbot to Moretonhampstead. Subsequently, in 1861, The Moretonhampstead and South Devon Railway Company (M&SDR) was formed with six directors including Thomas Wills of East Wrey and the Earl of Devon.

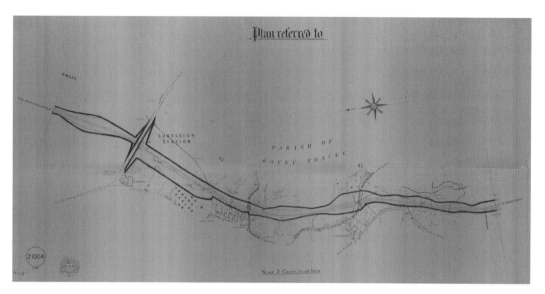

Plan referred to

British Railways Board plan of the railway through Lustleigh, c.1860.

Work began in 1863 and granite stones used in the construction of many of the bridges were cut and dressed from rocks on Lustleigh Cleave with horses and carts used to transport the stone from the Cleave to the building site. Additional granite, it is understood, was quarried at East Wrey and possibly also at Blackingstone and Knowle.[7] Anticipating a Board of Trade inspection, the branch line was ceremoniously opened on Tuesday 26th June 1866: such was the occasion that it was celebrated as a public holiday with crowds turning out to see the first train on its 12¼-mile journey from Newton Abbot to Moretonhampstead.

Initially, there were just two intermediate stations: at Bovey Tracey and Lustleigh; others were soon added at Teigngrace and Heathfield. Later a couple of halts were introduced, including Pullabrook (originally named Hawkmoor Halt but owing to the confusion of passengers disembarking thinking it was close to Hawkmoor tuberculosis sanatorium, it was renamed). In 1872 the M&SDR was fully amalgamated with the South Devon Railway which by the end of the decade had itself been absorbed into the Great Western Railway.

The railway brought many benefits to the people of Lustleigh, including employment; coal, building materials, animal feed, etc was transported more easily and quickly. Local produce reached wider markets. People travelled further afield, for business as well as pleasure. Men were employed in the teams maintaining the track, some were engine drivers, guards or firemen, and there was the station master and his staff.

"When it was a novelty here, our line had great attraction for young men and boys and many of them left their work on the land."
Cecil Torr, *Small Talk at Wreyland*

There were carriers who collected the goods that were brought to Lustleigh by the railway, while in the other direction rabbit-trappers, for example, used the rail to send their quarry from Lustleigh as far afield as the large Midland cities.

CLOCKWISE FROM TOP LEFT:
Lustleigh May Queen of 1936, Veronica Yeoman worked in the Ticket Office at the station; Luggage labels; Chudley's Delivery Cart outside the station.

Local businesses grew and prospered. There was a Post Office and General Stores, two butchers, two bakers and a coal merchant. With the increase in businesses and services, and the railway itself, there were more opportunities for employment at a time when farming was in decline.

There is no doubt, too, that the coming of the railway brought an increasing number of tourists to Lustleigh. Many private homes opened their doors to offer lodgings and in 1934, the GWR decided to equip 20 old coaches for use by campers and one was located in the sidings at Lustleigh. They generally slept six people.

Flowers and felines

Lustleigh Station became a very important place in the community - it was the place from where everyone came and went, where news came in from the outside world either by letter, telegraph, newspaper or by word of mouth.

In keeping with its role as one of the central hubs of the village, the station staff took great pride in tending its gardens which became renowned for being one of the best kept on the Great Western Railway. It often won prizes in the Best Station Garden competition run by the railway company; there is a suggestion that there may also have been allotments laid out on the opposite side of the tracks.

One who came to appreciate the setting was the station cat, Jumbo. His resting place was marked by a miniature gravestone bearing the inscription:

Beneath this slab
and stretched out flat,
lies Jumbo,
once our station cat.

Photograph courtesy of Bovey Tracey Heritage Centre

Lustleigh Station was used in the 1931[8] Sherlock Holmes' film of *The Hound of The Baskervilles*, produced by Gainsborough Pictures. The film starred Robert Rendell as Holmes who, coincidentally, was a past resident of the village, living for some time in "the big white house" near the station.[9] His co-star was Frederick Lloyd as Dr. Watson and the station was temporarily renamed "Baskerville".

Traces of the past

Relics of the old railway can still be found around the village: old track used as gateposts, for example, and one of the boundary marker stones is now a step in a local garden: of course, the bridges remain, not of all of them intact and most of them now on private land. The station is now a private house.

Some parts of the railway have been opened up as bridle and footpaths. The Wrey Valley Trail project utilises much of the old railway from Moretonhampstead to Lustleigh – and then onto Bovey Tracey – for walkers, cyclists and horse riders.

The End of the Line

From the beginning, the branch lines had always struggled financially. In the initial enthusiasm to promote the building of a line that was intended to bring prosperity to the local community, the cost of building routes over difficult terrain, of raising capital and of paying a huge workforce was largely underestimated. Many local lines found themselves unable to cover the normal running costs.

After the 1930s there was a steady decline in commercial activity. Smaller trades people left owing to competition from the larger shops and businesses in the growing nearby towns. The railway itself was running at a loss, the income from local traffic being insufficient to cover working expenses. With the increase in bus services and the use of the private motor car, the railway could no longer compete.

In May 1957, *The Mid-Devon Advertiser* revealed that the closure of the Moretonhampstead branch railway line was under consideration. In February 1959, the last passenger train came down the Moreton line to "whistle shrieks and Auld Lang Syne". Freight services continued for a few more years. After serving the needs of the local people for nearly a century the railway age for Lustleigh had come to an end.

The last train passes over the viaduct at Knowle.

3. Tourism

Picnic on the Cleave,
left Arthur Palk, 2nd left
Annie Palk (nee Easton).
Behind Annie is her
sister Laura Price.

For over two hundred years visitors have come to walk on Lustleigh Cleave in the protected landscapes of the Bovey Valley, to admire the thatched cottages around the medieval church and in nearby Wreyland, to stay in local accommodation and to refresh themselves physically in tea rooms, the café and the pub. Artists have been inspired by the landscapes, thousands of words, often superlatives, have been written to describe the parish and the tourist trade has provided employment for generations of Lustleigh residents.

Guide books have abounded in their praise of "the most charmingly situated village in Devon. The houses are scattered in very irregular and picturesque fashion, along the rugged bottom and steep sides of a little valley enclosed by high hills".[10] The abundance of granite in the parish also drawing attention such that "one would imagine that giants from Lustleigh Cleave had amused themselves with throwing rocks all over the place. There is granite in the gardens, granite in the fields, rocks crop up in the middle of the village, and seem strewn in every direction".[11]

Lustleigh Cleave

Although descriptions of the church and the Bishop's Stone are included in all entries in the guide books of the 19th and early 20th centuries, it was Lustleigh Cleave that elicited the most interest. The earliest guide book, *White's 1850 Devon Directory*, set the tone describing the Cleave as "a fine range of rocks and crags; and in the vicinity is a logan stone and some other Druidical remains."

Rather more lyrically, *Black's Guide to Devon SW, 1925* observed that "The glory of Lustleigh is its quite unrivalled Cleave, which may well be held the climax of all lovely scenery on the skins of Dartmoor... The

Rocky outcrop on Lustleigh Cleave.

sudden apparition of the glen is so startling in its loveliness that even the inhabitants have called it 'Heaven's Gate.'"

To get to the Cleave, the visitor arriving by train, guidebook in hand, would have walked through the village and turned right by the Baptist Chapel and taken the lane through Ellimore Farm, turning right again towards Hammerslake and taking the track that still leads on to the Cleave today. Alternatively, the walker may have turned left after Ellimore - an option offered in *Black's 1925 Guide* - and entered the Cleave at Heaven's Gate.

Another option for the visitor would be to hire a cab to take them up to the Cleave at Heaven's Gate where they might have spread their picnics out on the grass and enjoyed the view across the Cleave to Manaton and the moor beyond.

Postcard Chapman & Son

CLOCKWISE FROM TOP LEFT:
Charabanc outside Kelly Cottage; interior of Cleave Cottage at Hammerslake; Northpark Refreshment Bungalow at Hammerslake; May's Nursery and Tea Garden at Bishop's Stone.

Drink, eat & rest

The visitor may have stopped for refreshment at a tea garden, either of the 'pop-up' variety with people simply hanging a sign outside their house, or the more established watering holes at Cleave Cottage, Mead Head, Northpark (now Logan Stones), Broom Close (Copperwood) and at Caseley Nurseries, near the Bishop's Stone - handy for the Station. Refreshments would also have been available at the Cleave Hotel, formerly Gatehouse Farm, which opened in the mid-1860s to take advantage of the imminent arrival of the railway. The Cleave Hotel is the first place in the village to be recorded as offering accommodation.

According to records, the number of residences providing accommodation for the visitor has never been huge, being described in one guide book as "a sort of Chapel-of-Ease to Bovey as regards tourist accommodation".[12] It is likely that some houses offered bed and breakfast on an ad hoc basis from time to time - not all of it up to the standard expected by the visitor today!

"People crowd down here in summer," wrote Cecil Torr, "and will put up with any kind of lodging, as they mean to be out-doors all day. I have heard of rooms with "Wash in the Blood of the Lamb" in illuminated letters, where there should be a washstand. But this craze for rustic lodgings is comparatively new."[13]

By 1900, Kelly's and White's Directories were listing lodgings and furnished apartments at Caseley House, Cleaveland, Ellimore Farm, Grove Villa, Narramore, Orchard Villa and Rock Villa. Between the two World Wars, other places to stay included La Chaumiére, Oakhurst, Mill Cottage, Cleve House and Broom Close. In the 1940s, East Wrey Barton had opened as a guest house and bed and breakfast was being offered at North Harton Farm, while the 1959 edition of the Lustleigh Guide carried adverts for accommodation at St. Andrew's, Parklands and Moorwood Cottage. 'Alternative' places to stay have included a temperance hotel, opposite The Cleave Hotel and now called Brookside, and a vegetarian guest house run by Mrs Read at Cleave Lodge.

BOTTOM LEFT:
The Cleave Hotel with Brookside in the foreground.

BOTTOM RIGHT:
Long term landlords of The Cleave Hotel, Scott and Lillian Painter.

A modern day view of The Cleave "The Only Pub in the Village".

Glamping

In 1934, the Great Western Railway positioned one of their camping coaches at Lustleigh Station. With accommodation for six people, the holiday coach remained in use until 1958, except for ten years or so during and after the Second World War. To further encourage business on their lines, GWR also published guide books over many years, including "Glorious Devon" first published in 1928. An extract from that edition describes the scenery getting "rapidly more beautiful as we climb up the wooded valley to Lustleigh, where huge granite boulders lie all over the steep hillsides... Lustleigh Cleave, a narrow steep wooded valley, two miles long, is like an Isle of Wight chine on a much wider scale, full of queer-shaped rocks with names like the Round of Beef, Nutcracker, and Gate of Heaven".[14]

With the increase in visitors, sometimes their behaviour became something to comment on. As early as July 1898, the editor of the Parish Magazine was hoping that "the Tourists who come to Lustleigh will not take away all the ferns and wild plants and flowers they admire, some of which they throw away". Most, though, just left with indelible memories: from 1916 until at least the mid-20s, Lustleigh Station kept a visitors' book, and one visitor used poetry to express their delight:

> *I've spent a day and ere I leave,*
> *A word of praise for Lustleigh Cleave,*
> *Char-a-banc parties crane their necks.*
> *The short-sighted ones don their specs — and marvel.*

Of course, other forms of transport were also bringing visitors to the village. Lustleigh became a popular destination for coach parties, including evening 'mystery tours' from Torquay and Teignmouth. Indeed, coaches have been bringing visitors to Lustleigh since at least 1900 when Hellier & Lee ran coach excursions from Bovey Tracey that included a "...*return by the Swiss like scenery of the Lustleigh valley*". At times there could be up to five coaches parked in the centre of the village, although on one summer evening in the 1960s, there were as many as 17.

Cars were also on the increase and in the late 1920s and early 30s, visitors were being advised to park on the green by the church steps "under the elms" and walk to Lustleigh Cleave: the road beyond the village "being unsuitable for motor vehicles."

Visitors would also look around the centre of the

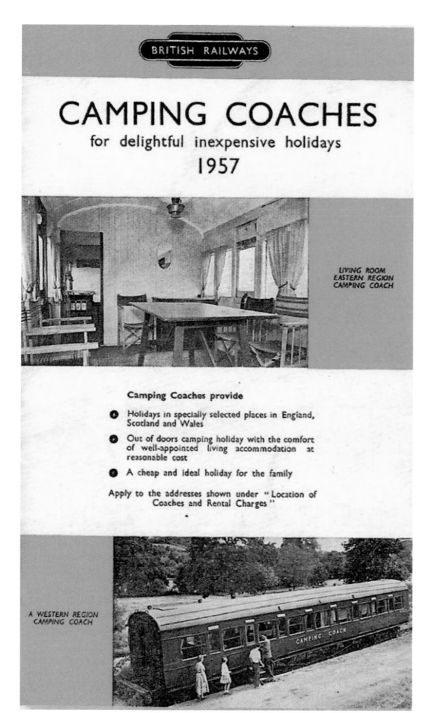

village, walk across to Wreyland and then sample the delights of The Cleave Hotel and The Primrose Tea Rooms where, at times, people queued up outside - even in the rain! The Primrose, built in the 1940s on the site of a lean-to store for the adjacent grocery shop, has been a draw in itself: at the height of its fame in the 1980s, visitors came from as far away as America and Europe to sample its cakes and cream teas, and it was catering for up to 300 people a day.

The village's heyday for tourism was in the 1920s, 30s and in the first 25 years after the Second World War. Although the number of visitors was falling by the 1980s, the village remains a popular destination for all-comers whether arriving by car, bicycle or Shanks's pony.

4. Manor and Farms

Few records exist to inform us about the early histories of the various farms in Lustleigh. According to the Domesday Book, the manor comprised a demesne farm of about 200 acres and eleven villein farms averaging about 70 acres a piece. From various accounts, it is believed that the demesne farm, that which belonged to the Lord of the Manor and where, for example, the manorial courts were held, was Barne, later known as Barncourt.[15] As for the eleven others, it is thought that seven of these would have been those listed in the Devonshire Lay Subsidy of 1332, namely Pepperdon, Caseley, Foxworthy, Boveycombe,

Lussacombe with Ash House in the foreground.

Pethybridge, Harton and Mapstone. It is unclear which the remainder would have been other than they were likely to have been four from Rudge, Peck, Combe, Waye, Ellimore, Hisley and Fursdon.

Surveys of the Manor of Lustleigh in 1615 and 1626 provide us with details of all the existing farms and cottages, their occupiers, acreage and rental value. From this time onwards it is possible to trace occupation and ownership virtually unbroken for each house and farm to the present day.

From the 1615 survey, it is possible to deduce some of the developments which had previously taken place: we see, for example, that Combe farm had been split in three with Lower, Middle and Higher Combe now listed; Hisley had been divided into Higher and Lower Hisley; Harton had also been split in two with North and South Harton. We also see the possible appearance of newer farms such as Lussacombe, North Narramore and East Wrey.

The survey further reveals that Caseley was, at that time, twinned with another farm known as Stockner; this latter, however, ceased to be a farm around 1850 and traces of its remains can be found near the route of the old railway line about a mile from Lustleigh in the direction of Moretonhampstead.

A more significant ruin is that of Boveycombe in Hisley Woods which was abandoned much more recently, probably in the 1940s when, according to oral history, the last person to have farmed there was George Crocker who grew potatoes. The buildings have been dated as 14th century, so whether the farm does in fact pre-date the Devonshire Lay Subsidy of 1332 is unclear. The various manorial surveys do, though, give us information as to occupation with William Grose holding it in 1615, Nicholas Gray in residence in 1628 and Gilbert Babbacome farming its 33 acres in 1742. The farm remained in the same family until the 1837 Tithe Map shows it in the ownership of John Gould, and occupied by George Wills, the total acreage now recorded as being 69 and a half acres.

The Wills family were, at one time, one of the principal landowners in the village, becoming established here in the 15th century. George Wills was one of three men in 1630 to each buy a quarter of the manor which they then proceeded to split among themselves with the Wills family getting Higher Combe, Higher Hisley, Rudge, East Wrey, Pethybridge, Lower Hisley, Lussacombe, Gatehouse and North Harton. Records are said to show that George was descended from tenants on the Wreyland Court Rolls of 1437 ; also that Wreyland was once part of the same manor as Lustleigh before it was split off, only to come back into the fold in the last century. Records also show a Wills as a freeholder at Vinnemore (another ruin close to Boveycombe) at the beginning of the 17th century.

Some of the former Wills' farms are no longer recognisable as former farmsteads. In particular, Pethybridge has evolved into more of a hamlet: one of the descendants, John Wills, sold off much of the farmland in 1886 for houses (possibly connected with the arrival of the railway) and more land was sold in 1934 for the building of council houses. Gatehouse was also affected by the coming of the railway, in its case being transformed into the Cleave Hotel.

Rudge, by contrast, remained within the family for over 200 years. At his death in 1691, George Wills owned two-thirds of Rudge, one quarter of which he inherited and the remainder he purchased, with his great grandson acquiring the remaining third in 1805. The farm passed after two more generations to the childless widow of George in 1873 and then out of the Wills family.[16] At one time, the Rudge estate included two mills, one of which still exists.

The Wills family were also connected with Caseley. Before the manor of Lustleigh was broken up, the farmstead had been owned by the Caseleigh family, (its most likely original spelling), but through successive marriages it came into the possession of George Wills in 1808, later being owned by Thomas Wills of East Wrey who was also owner of Gatehouse.

Boundary changes have affected the farming landscape of the parish as mentioned in the opening chapter on the history of the village, with the loss of Pepperdon and the addition of Sanduck in 1885. The parish was further enlarged in 1957 with the addition of the ancient manor of Wreyland which incorporated both Knowle and Kelly and previously fell within Bovey Tracey's boundary.

Six of the farms owned
by the Wills family.

**THIS PAGE,
CLOCKWISE FROM
TOP LEFT:**
Caseley, Waye and
Pethybridge.

**OPPOSITE PAGE,
CLOCKWISE FROM
TOP LEFT:**
Rudge (rebuilt probably
after a serious fire),
Willmead and Higher
Hisley in 1900.

CLOCKWISE FROM TOP LEFT: Wreyland is a small hamlet of closely clustered thatched buildings, among them Lower Wreyland, Yonder Wreyland (this particular image shows the original building before it was destroyed by fire) and Wreyland Manor.

Postcard F. Frith & Co

With regard to Wreyland, during the 18th century most of its land was also concentrated into the ownership of the Wills family, although at that time the Lordship of the Manor of Wreyland was held by Nelson Beveridge Gribble who lived at Knowle and owned some 200 acres. Although his son sold Knowle and most of the land, the family retained a house called Yonder Wreyland; this later passed to the sister of a John Gribble who was married to James Tarr, an ironmonger of Moretonhampstead. His son entered the legal profession and changed his name to Torr and his grandson was Cecil Torr, the scholar, barrister, author and local historian.

Knowle was the seat of another family which became significant landowners in Lustleigh. Francis Daniell, who had bought Knowle in 1797 sold it to John Gould in 1825 who, six years later, added Lower Hisley and Boveycombe to his estate.

Amery is another of Lustleigh's major farming families. In the 17th century, Nicholas Amery of Bridford married the daughter of a tenant farmer at Middle Combe; another Amery, tenant of North Harton in the late 17th century, married into the Sparke family of Ellimore. For the next two hundred years the Amery family continued to purchase other farms in the parish. Kelly Farm is the last remaining farm to be owned by an Amery, although this was also once in the hands of the Wills family, including the formative years of the 'Shiny Ore' mine there.

When an act of parliament in 1805 enabled the Wyndham family to divest themselves of their one third of the manor, their shares were bought principally by the farm occupiers who were finally in a position to own 100 per cent of their properties. The records show that, at that point, the Amery family owned some 10 properties (including Mapstone,

Middle Wreyland when it was a few small cottages.

Barncourt, Higher Combe[17], Lower Combe, Narramore[18], Middle Combe, Hammerslake, North Harton, Newton Peck and Ellimore) with a similar number in the hands of the Wills family. Indeed, there were only four farms that were independently owned at that point: Boveycombe, East Fursdon, West Fursdon and Waye.

In addition to the mills on the Rudge estate, there was also a mill at Foxworthy. Like nearly all mills at that time it was a water mill and it was driven by the River Bovey. It was obviously of importance to farms such as Peck, Barncourt, Fursdon, Narramore and North Harton and of course Foxworthy as it was nearer to these farms than Lustleigh Mill. Foxworthy Mill was dismantled in 1878 and replaced by the present house in 1891.

Postcard Chapman & Son

CLOCKWISE FROM TOP LEFT: Some of the Amery farms and tenements. Lower Combe; Kelly Cottage; Higher Combe; a rare image of Barn Court (a facsimile of a painting owned by the Amery family) of which there is now little trace, apart from the perimeter wall.

© Crown copyright. Historic England Archive

The Great
Hall exterior.

It is worth a note on The Great Hall which some believe was originally the manor house and is, indeed, sometimes referred to as The Old Manor House. There is little doubt that it is one of the oldest buildings in the parish with many of its timbers being dated to around the 14th century. However, as the manorial records inform us, the principal building of the manor was Barne, or Barncourt. A more likely title, centuries past, may have been the Old Rectory Manor, having been given by a previous Lord to the church some time between 1200 and 1600. It continued as the rectory until 1926[19] after which the rector's residence was transferred to a more modern building, now known as the

The Great Hall, view of the Solar.

Old Rectory at the bottom of Mapstone Hill. The Great Hall, containing two of the most interesting medieval roofs in Devon, has since been divided into three dwellings.

It would possibly be remiss to close this chapter without a mention of Lustleigh Cleave which would have been considered as the 'manorial waste land', that is to say that it could not provide for cultivation but could be used for rough grazing and wood, turf or peat, stones and gravel, and acorns. In 1626/28, common rights to the 300 or so acres of Bovicombe Cleeve (as it was known then[20]) were given to Fursdon, Ellimore, Boveycombe, Higher Hisley, Pethybridge, North Harton, Peck, Waye, Higher Combe, Middle Combe and Lower Combe.

At various times, there have been disputes over who has rights over this land including a prosecution against poachers in 1887. More recently, though, several developments took place following a government act in 1966 aiming to register all common land. At the conclusion of that exercise, it was decided that ownership rested with the Public Trustee, but with 'beneficial owners' being the owners of Foxworthy and Higher Combe along with two previous owners of one third of the manor, the Wyndhams and the Strangeways (now Lord Ilchester). Additionally, however, there are around 40 commoners who have certain rights on the Cleave.

As a footnote, it should be added that Trendlebere Down was also shared common land with Lower Hisley and Rudge holding the 'moiety' of this 200-acre patch of Dartmoor; today it is owned and managed by Natural England, but with a number of commoners having rights here too.

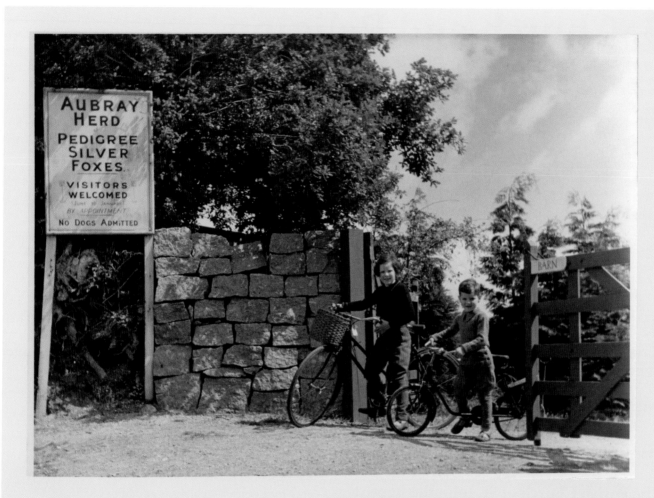

Cothland Barn at Hammerslake was a farm of a different sort for Lustleigh. The owners ran it as a Silver Fox Fur farm and according to the sign welcomed visitors from June to January.
The children are Jennifer and David Short.

5. Church and Religion

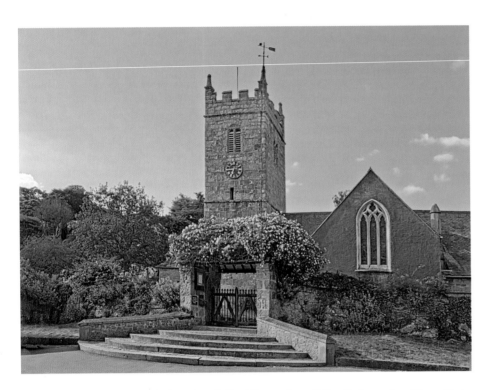

The Parish Church of St. John the Baptist

Lustleigh's parish church, situated in a circular enclosed graveyard, undoubtedly stands on the site of an earlier building, possibly consisting of a simple oblong room made of wood or cob with a thinly thatched roof. By the Saxon era, there may have been a more substantial stone building which was developed in Norman times; there is Norman cable-moulding on the font.

Our parish church incorporates many of the later styles of church architecture. The original structure is of the Early English style, being built between 1180 and 1280, and consisted of a chancel, nave and south porch. The simple lancet windows in the chancel, the double piscina and the three sedilia are from this period. The first addition came in the early 14th century when the lord of the manor, Sir William le Prous[21], built the south chapel as his mortuary chapel. His effigy is seen there today.

The church tower was added in the Perpendicular period, between 1400 and 1500. By the end of the 15th century, the population of Lustleigh must have increased to make it necessary to add a north aisle. The original north wall was removed and pillars were built to support the roof.

Church Bells

Lustleigh's bells have summoned people to worship throughout the ages: the inscription on the second bell reads: "When I call Follow all". Originally there were four bells; a treble was added in 1875 and a tenor in 1890, both having been cast by Taylors of Loughborough, founders of the "Great Paul" of St. Paul's Cathedral. Our bells have been rung over the centuries for weddings, deaths, coronations and national celebrations. The ringers' valuable contribution to the life and work of the church and parish has always been appreciated in the past and still is today.

One of Lustleigh's oldest houses, The Great Hall on Mapstone Hill (noted for its 14th century roof timbers)

Bell Ringers 1936, from left to right, Sylvester Morecombe, George Morecombe, Tom Payne, Mark Germon, Lewin Hill, Jacob Wright.

TOP:
Rev. Ensor, Rector
1847 – 1887.

BELOW:
The Rood Screen.

was the Rectory from before 1600 until well into the 20th century. The Rev. William Davy came to live in the Rectory in 1785 as Curate-in-Charge. During his 40 years here, his contribution to improving the life of his parishioners was considerable, building the first school in Lustleigh and founding the Davy Charity. He also built a printing press and printed 26 volumes of his sermons.

For more than 700 years, from 1262 to 1985, there was an unbroken succession of Rectors. Following the retirement of the Rev. Edwin Deacon in 1985, the Rev. Kenneth E. Jackson was appointed "Priest in Charge" and from the time of his retirement in 1995, Lustleigh has ceased to have its own resident parson. Our parish church is now part of the United Benefice of Moretonhampstead, Manaton, North Bovey and Lustleigh.

CLOCKWISE FROM TOP LEFT:
Choir Boys 1953 from left to right, Michael Price, John Price, Raymond Squires, David Williams, Michael Linsell, David Price; The Font; View of church from Mapstone Hill; Church Interior, showing fresco painted to celebrate Queen Victoria's Diamond Jubilee.

Postcard F. Frith & Co

The Church House

Lustleigh, like so many other parishes in the country, has its own Church House, built around the mid-15th century probably by public subscription. Church House was used for many church and social occasions as well as having been a parish poorhouse in the 19th century. In 1888, it was remodelled to include a parish room in memory of Rev. Frederic Ensor, rector for over 40 years. In more recent times it has been used as a Reading Room, a meeting room, a school and for a private commercial business. Many ancient Church Houses have disappeared over the centuries; it is fortunate for Lustleigh that this beautiful old building has survived.

The Roman Catholic Chapel

In the 1950s, Roman Catholics in Lustleigh were able to worship together in a private chapel built by Mrs. Dolly Walmesly next to her home at Pixies' Cottage (now Higher Hill) on Mapstone Hill. There was a small organ to accompany the congregation of 15 to 20, who were supported in the celebration of Mass by Dom Rafael Stone, a monk at Buckfast Abbey.

When Mrs. Walmesly sold and left Pixies' Cottage in 1984, there was no other place to meet and so Roman Catholic worship in Lustleigh came to an end.

Two images of the Church House showing the modern day building and a painting of the building when it was thatched dating from 1886.

Courtesy of The Museum of English Rural Life, Reading

Lustleigh Baptist Chapel

In 1809 and 1835, licenses were given to the dissenting Christians of Lustleigh to meet in named houses which were then registered as Meeting Houses. The land for the erection of a chapel was purchased in May 1853 for the sum of £5.5s (£5.25p). It is not known who built the chapel; possibly it was the members of the congregation themselves. The chapel, situated at the bottom of Ellimore Hill, has always had its own graveyard.

The Baptists continued to flourish, and by the 1950s had a Sunday school and Sunshine Corner for the young, though lack of space was always a problem. From the 1980s, there have been significant improvements to the original building.

In 1976, the three congregations of Lustleigh, Bovey Tracey and Moretonhampstead became the East Dartmoor Baptist Church, with the addition of Chudleigh in 1977 and Christow in 1986. However, they reverted to independent status in 2010.

Gospel Hall and Plymouth Brethren

Early meetings of the Plymouth Brethren in Lustleigh were held in private homes until Mrs. Whiteside allowed the Assembly to use the building at the foot of the village green for worship. In 1971, the building was offered for sale to the congregation who were able to arrange the purchase thanks to a large donation by one of their members. The building is no longer used on a regular basis, but at one time the Plymouth Brethren were a significant part of Lustleigh's religious life.

Many people from outside areas attended 'Revivalist' meetings and "We village children, whether chapel or church, were made welcome at the service, and oh! the thrill of joining in the singing, with the men's thunderous bass voices of "You must be a lover of the Lord Jesus Christ, or you won't go to heaven when you die!" - or the gentler "Jesus wants me for a sunbeam"."[22]

6. Working Life

Working on a farm on a hill above the village, location and date unknown.

Hugh Chudley delivering dairy produce from Ellimore Farm c.1930.

Farming

"Before the railway brought outsiders in, there was hardly anybody in the place who did not own land or rent it or work on it"
Cecil Torr 'Small Talk at Wreyland, Vol II'

For many centuries working life in Lustleigh was mainly centred around farming. This is reflected in the 1851 census which listed 10 farmers and 43 farm labourers among the 51 households; there were also carpenters, blacksmiths and a wheelwright, all of whom would have been employed on the local farms, along with an array of farm servants.

Mostly, there were small hill farms with a mix of animals - cattle, pigs, sheep and poultry - while some of those on the more productive land were able to grow wheat, barley, potatoes and peas. There were also many orchards, growing apples for eating but more especially for cider making; almost every farm had its own cider press.

Although the railway opened up new markets for farm produce in the 19th century, the small farms could not compete with those in the more fertile areas elsewhere and the industry went into decline. Many farmhouses were sold off and became separated from the land, which now is generally down to pasture, usually grazed by sheep and horses.

In the years following the First World War, employment was provided in the commercial planting of trees in the Wray and Bovey valleys.

Clog making

Perhaps one of the most unusual uses of the land prior to the war was in the production of an item not normally associated with Devon – clogs. According to the February 1889 issue of Lustleigh parish magazine, "Five men and two boys under Mr. Goodfellow's direction, are cutting down alder trees, to make them into wooden shoes or clogs… By the end of March six months will have passed … and probably about 50,000 pairs will have been sent in trucks from Lustleigh Station to Manchester. The wood, when cut into the required shape… is stacked to dry for three weeks or a month, and the shoes when finished with leather tops [back in Lancashire] are used by mill hands, people working in factories and collieries etc." The clogs would cost around 4 shillings and 6 pence (22½p) to 5 shillings for men, 3s 6d – 4s for women and 2s 6d – 3s 6d for children; they would last about a year, although could be 'rebottomed' with fresh wood. How long this industry lasted is unknown.

Mills and Bakeries

From medieval times, almost every manor had its own grist mill to which the farmers were required to bring their corn. Reference to the mill at Lustleigh is found in documents as early as 1316. From 1600, it was part of the Rudge estate and continued to be so until 1961. There was also a mill at the northern end of the parish at Foxworthy.

In the 17th and 18th centuries, the mill was an essential part of the farming industry and the miller was an important (though not always respected) member of the local community. By the mid-19th century, however, the fortunes of the small mill at Lustleigh were in decline due to competition from other larger mills outside the parish. Around 1870,

The Mill, Lustleigh

a bakery was built in an attempt to revive business at the mill and the owners, Samuel Dart at least, would ensure that customers would receive their

The Mill, by Thomas Rowden, Watercolour, 1886.

bread whatever the obstacle. "On Monday March 9th, the snow which most people thought would not be seen again this winter, returned… many roads were impassable, a Blizzard, that is a storm of wind and fine snow, raged for hours… Bread through the bravery of bakers was supplied, and Mr. Dart, and his man and boy happily live to tell the tale that they went from Lustleigh Mill to North Bovey, Barne, and Peck, with bags of loaves on their backs, and came back the same day."

Baking at Lustleigh mill continued throughout the First World War but by then a new bakery had been built at Brookfield. By 1906 Lustleigh mill was described in the Ordnance Survey map as "disused". The bakery at Brookfield went on producing bread until the early 1980s when, like the mill, it became a private house.

One villager, John Dray remembers that the bakery at Brookfield "had a donkey which pulled a small cart delivering bread and I recall on numerous occasions hearing yells from the baker when the wretched beast, half way up Mapstone Hill, decided to go home hell for leather."[23]

The Osborne Family outside the bakery in Brookfield.

Charles and Brenda Osborne with the donkey cart.

Kelly Mine Workforce c.1907
Left to right, Bill Martin, Jabez Hill, Ernest Squires, Bill Squires (possibly), unknown, Alf Martin (possibly), John Johns.

Mining and Quarrying

As happened all over Dartmoor, tin mining took place in Lustleigh in the 15th and 16th centuries, though there is very little evidence left of this activity. Much more important in recent times has been the mining of micaceous haematite, or 'shiny ore', found at various sites along the Wrey Valley.

"In the parishes of Hennock and Lustleigh, there is found in the granite a species of micaceous or peculiar iron-ore, known by the name of Devonshire Sand… used for writing sand and various other purposes."[24] At one time, it was "sold to the colour makers to add to the weight of their paints"[25] and it became very important in Victorian times as a corrosion-resistant base in paint for ships and bridges. It was also used in the glazing process at the local potteries.

'Shiny Ore', so named because of the metallic sparkle of iron oxide within, was mined at Kelly, situated at the eastern edge of Lustleigh, providing employment for six to eight workers at a wage higher than that of agricultural labourers, though the risks were greater. As well as the miners, there were surface workers who sorted, washed

and packed the ore, and a blacksmith who sharpened the drills and picks. The full barrels were loaded on to carts or lorries and taken to Lustleigh Station.

Small scale production at Kelly Mine went on from the late 18th century and from 1900 output was greatly increased. However, in 1951, there was a collapse in the Slade workings at the mine which resulted in the closure of all the operations in the Wray Valley. Today the Kelly Mine Preservation Society is working to restore the mine, and to research its history and it has been described as "one of the finest examples of preserved rural industry in the country".[26]

There was also work in the granite quarries in the Wray Valley and at Moretonhampstead. Villager, Bill Squires remembers: "The local stone quarries provided good work as did the silver [sic] ore mine at Kelly. My father was a 'blaster' in both quarries, being paid for the material he produced after each firing…. The explosive used was industrial dynamite ignited by a fuse and detonator."

Gardening

There was always plenty of gardening work for Lustleigh men and boys. The many large houses, particularly those built in the 19th and early 20th centuries, were generally owned by the well-to-do who were able to employ a full-time gardener and sometimes two. In the period after the First World War the wage was around £1. 10s (£1.50) to £2 per week.

There were several market gardens in Lustleigh in the 20th century. One of these, on the corner of Caseley road was run by Mr. and Mrs. May who also ran a tea room for visitors. Boveycombe Flower Farm at Lower Hisley was owned by the Gould family who grew potatoes in Boveycombe Field (now lost in the woods on Lustleigh Cleave) during the Second World War.

Jim Knight at Lussacombe 1944.

Miss Phillis Collett at Foxworthy with milk pails c.1907.

Clara Chudley helps with the potato harvest, Mapstone Hill, 1943.

Women's work

For the women and young girls, the major source of employment was found in the village shops or in the large houses and guest houses as housekeepers, maids, cleaners etc. As a young boy, Bill Squires found work at the Cleave Hotel as a general "dogsbody" living in six and a half days a week for five shillings. Two other female employees lived-in, one was "a pretty, black-haired young girl" called Norah Hatherley: "she was full of fun and looked quite stunning in her black dress and white apron". She was the general assistant and waitress for serving table.

> "I had to be down in that kitchen at 7 o'clock in a morning, clean out the range, clean the flues every morning. It was two flues we had, 'twas the double oven, and when you cleaned that fireplace, the range, you had to see your face in it, 'twas like silver when you'd cleaned it... I never used to go to bed till ten to half past and in the summer time, when we had people in, I was up about six and went to bed half past eleven because we had to do everything, we had to clean the shoes of a morning, I had to bring all the shoes down..."
>
> *Mrs Norah Wright (née Hatherley b.1914)*

From the second half of the 20th century, with the decline in farming and mining, the loss of the railway and the closing down of shops and businesses, these opportunities for employment have either disappeared or are strictly limited. Many working people must now commute to Exeter or Plymouth or the neighbouring towns, while others work from home.

Postcard F. Frith & Co

Shops

Looking around the village today, it is hard to visualise the hive of retail activity that buzzed around the green and close by: today we have just The Cleave, Primrose Tea Room and The Dairy, but in days gone by, so much more was available.

Tracking the history of the Post Office alone gives a sense of how Lustleigh's retail environment has changed. Initially, there was just a post office receiver, and in the 1860s that was Louisa Smallridge, wife of a blacksmith. Later, another blacksmith, John Bennett became a postmaster who passed the business onto his son-in-law William Bartlett, in 1890[27]. William operated from Stable House which was situated at right angles to the Primrose, although at that point it wasn't a tea room, just a single-story building which probably functioned as a store to the shop. Immediately upon taking up his position, William enlarged the shop front with a bay window, no doubt with a view to growing the accompanying grocery business: certainly, an application for a Post Office Savings Bank was applied for along with a facility to receive telegrams.

Around the 1920s, the Post Office moved into purpose-built premises (originally called Claremont) and, in 1928, William passed the business to his son-in-law, Robert Beer[28], who continued until his retirement in 1948, ending a family connection with the Post Office which had lasted over 70 years. As with many rural villages, the Post Office closed in 2009 and postal facilities were taken over by The Dairy opposite.

The shop now housing The Dairy has had its own chequered history. For many years, at the end of the Victorian era and before WW1, it was run by Percy William Peters who sold all manner of groceries as well as wine and spirits. Later it became a Co-Op stores before returning to an independent grocery. Then, it too was faced with closure before being saved by a village consortium which now owns the building and rents it out on a non-commercial basis.

Over the decades, the village has also had butchers, bakers, a sweet shop at Columbine, a second-hand shop in Pound Barn and a gallery/gift shop in the original post office building at Stable House; at one time, there was also another grocery store in Brookfield which housed a small café. All of these now, though, are at best distant memories or otherwise simply dusty records.

TOP LEFT TO RIGHT: Peters Stores, now Lustleigh Dairy; Bibbings Stores and the building which is now Primrose Tea Rooms; Lustleigh Post Office 1920.

CLOCKWISE FROM TOP RIGHT:
Road gang working at Sanduck; Local Gamekeeper Tim Raisey; a group of building workers at a local property or mine; c.1920s; G R Dray and Son (Mick Dray) re-thatching No 2 Pound Cottages.

Photograph courtesy of Len Harvey

CLOCKWISE FROM TOP LEFT:
PC Doble and family outside the Police House in Brookfield, 1943; Nick Wotton in the sorting office at Lustleigh c.2009 shortly before it closed, John Maymon Harris outside his boot & shoe business c.1900.

7. Celebrations & Commemorations

Mabel Bunclark the first May Queen after it was resurrected by Cecil Torr in 1905.

May Day

May Day has been celebrated in Lustleigh for over a hundred years. Although maypole dancing had taken place "at the flower show and other festivals" previously, in 1905 Cecil Torr started the May Day festival. Until 1940 the crowning of the May Queen took place on the hillside above Wreyland at Long Tor Farm (now on private land), where the names of May Queens are carved on a granite boulder. After a break between 1941 and 1953, when the ceremony didn't take place, the celebration was revived in 1954 with the main event held in the Town Orchard.

Today, every year on the first Saturday in May, the celebration begins with a procession around the village. A magnificent canopy of flowers is carried over the May Queen by four canopy bearers. The May Queen is followed by the children of the village carrying bunches of flowers. The procession pauses at various points around the village for the children to sing traditional May carols before stopping at the Church Steps where the May Queen is blessed by the Rector. The procession then moves into the orchard where the Queen is crowned on the May Day Rock and the children dance around the Maypole.

The old May
Rock at Long Tor.

CLOCKWISE FROM TOP LEFT:
1922, Phyllis Yeoman with the parade at Wreyland Manor; Gillian Williams May Day 1954, the Queen is now crowned on the new rock in the Orchard; the children assemble for the start of the parade in the playground of the school, Iona Jones in 1960.

CLOCKWISE FROM TOP LEFT:
Wendy Harvey in 1971; Celebrating 110 Years of May Day in 2015, Rev. Simon Franklin blessing the crowd; Amy Jaggs, May Queen 2017.

Lustleigh Show

The Lustleigh Show, held on August Bank Holiday Monday, is the largest annual event to be held in the village. The event started in 1887 as the Cottage Garden Exhibition and held in conjunction with the annual fete of the Rational Sick and Burial Association. In the early days, exhibitors concentrated their efforts on vegetables and fruit - in 1888, over 2,000 potatoes (of all sorts and sizes) were on display and flowers, 'lent for decoration by the resident gentry', were used to adorn the tent.

Under the auspices of the Lustleigh Horticultural Society, the event continued until 1990 when it was taken over by a dedicated Lustleigh Show committee. The format of the Show as we know it today, on fields belonging to Kelly Farm, developed in the years after the Second World War. A gymkhana and dog show were soon added and, for a number of years, one of the most important goat shows in the region, attracting entries from all over the South West, was held as part of the Lustleigh Show. In recent years, the Show, with the Horticultural Show, gymkhana, sideshows, cross country running, and arena events, has attracted over 3,000 visitors annually.

LUSTLEIGH

FETE & ATHLETIC SPORTS.

MONDAY, August 1st. 1892.

A PROGRAMME AND LIST OF PRIZES.

Race for Boys under 14	3/-	2/-	1/-
One Mile Race	10/-	5/-	2/6
High Jump	10/-	5/-	2/6
Two Hundred Yards Race	5/-	3/-	2/-
Long Jump	5/-	3/-	2/-
Hurdle Race, 10 flights 200 yards,	7/6	5/-	2/6
Tug of War	15/-		
Race for Girls under 14	3/-	2/-	1/-
Race for Young Men under 20	3/-	2/-	1/-
Three-legged Race	5/-	3/-	2/-
Egg and Spoon Race		2/-	1/-
Veteran Race for Men over 40	5/-	3/-	2/-
Boys eating Biscuits	1/6		6d.

All Events open. The decision of the Judge to be final.
The Committee reserve the right to make any minor alterations necessary.

CLOCKWISE FROM TOP RIGHT:
Early Show poster from 1892;
after-show auction with Dave Wills;
The Horticultural Show marquee.

Parishioners take a rest
(probably at Horsham
Steps) while Beating
the Bounds.

Beating the Bounds

The tradition of beating the bounds, still observed in many Dartmoor parishes, is believed to be based on an ancient ritual in which the knowledge of parish boundaries was handed down the generations and checks were made to ensure that their lands had not been encroached upon by neighbouring parishes.

The early history of the custom in Lustleigh is unclear, but it certainly stuttered its way through the first half of the 20th century, being revived once in 1924 after a lapse (of unknown duration), then again in 1950 following an 18-year lapse when, in September 'a goodly number of parishioners

assembled at the Clam Bridge on the River Bovey to walk around the second half of the parish boundary, the first half being completed earlier in the year'.[29]

In May 1957, a special event was held to mark the extension of the parish boundary, when 460 acres of land including Kelly, Brookfield, Knowle, Yeo and Wreyland passed from Bovey Tracey to Lustleigh. However, only the new section of the parish was walked on that occasion. Finally, in 1975, the current practice of beating the bounds of the enlarged parish was introduced and has been carried out every 5 years since then.

CLOCKWISE FROM TOP
The custom of "bumping" the youngest parishioner at various points to make sure they remember the boundary for the future; walking the old railway between Lustleigh and Moretonhampstead - 1950's; crossing fields above Moretonhampstead in 2010.

Royal celebrations

In 1863, 'the little parish of Lustleigh was all alive with loyalty' for the wedding of the Prince of Wales and Princess Alexandra of Denmark where the morning began 'with the ringing of bells, firing of guns and [sound of] blacksmiths' anvils'. Over 400 people attended, the men enjoying 'substantial food and cider', the women and children 'a plentiful supply of tea and currant cake', followed by 'rural sports and dancing'.[30] For the marriage of the Duke of York and Princess Mary in 1893, every child was presented with a medal and then processed to 'Petherbridge Moor' [sic] for 'an excellent tea' and sports, while those in receipt of parish relief were given half-a-crown each.

Naturally, the milestones of Victoria's reign followed the same enthusiastic pattern, her Golden Jubilee (1887) celebrated with the usual 'repast of beef, plum-pudding and one quart of cider given to all males above fourteen years of age' while 'for the women an excellent high tea was given'[31]; the lych gate and church steps were also built to mark the occasion. Similar festivities attended Victoria's Diamond Jubilee (1897) and her eightieth birthday (1899), with her death in 1901, after a reign of over 63 years, being marked only with 'the Church bells tolled late in the evening'.

Lustleigh villagers assemble in their finery to mark Queen Victoria's Golden Jubilee.

CLOCKWISE FROM TOP LEFT:
George VI Street Party 1937; Queen Elizabeth II Diamond Jubilee sundial; local children perform "Wee Willie Winkie" for Queen Elizabeth II's coronation.

Since then, of course, Queen Elizabeth II surpassed Victoria as the longest reigning monarch giving at least as much opportunity for royal celebrations. In familiar style, a bonfire on the Cleave rounded off the celebrations of Elizabeth's coronation, the day having included children's sports, maypole dancing and an evening dance in the Conservative Hall. Several days of celebrations marked her silver jubilee in 1977 including a carnival, while for her golden jubilee, the activities ranged from a barbecue and a disco to a specially written 'Jubilee Cantata' by local composer, Will Carnell. As a lasting legacy, Elizabeth's 60 years on the throne were marked by a vertical sundial installed on the southern wall of the Old Vestry.

Other milestones

There have, of course, been other events in the lives of Lustleigh folk which have been worthy of celebration. The coming of the railway was a momentous occasion as evidenced by a newspaper article which remarked that 'the whole parish of Lustleigh numbers less than 500 inhabitants, yet £40 was collected for the purpose of giving a handsome treat to "one and all"... Two large marquees were erected' where 'a cold collation was served up to all the labouring men of the parish'. This was followed by 'donkey racing, foot racing, wrestling, dancing' opened by 'four Lustleigh [old] boys whose united ages amounted to 310 years' and topped with a 'splendid tea'.[32]

More recently, the village celebrated the transition from the second to the third millennium with a variety of events. First, on 31 December 1999, there was a celebration of Christianity in the church involving music, hymns and readings from

parishioners, followed by mulled wine, a torch-lit procession around the village centre and concluding with fireworks in the cricket field. The following day, commemorative millennium glass tankards, kindly produced by the House of Marbles, were distributed to 129 children of the parish under the age of 18.

The May Day Rock in the Town Orchard.

May 2000 was marked by the appearance of two special granite memorials. The first was a new throne for the May Queen, designed by local architect, Doug Cooper, carved out of granite from Blackenstone[33] Quarry by master mason, Warren Pappas and unveiled by Lustleigh's oldest surviving May Queen, Mrs Nell Squires. The second was a 'Millennium Rock', a new boundary stone sited close to where the parish boundary emerges from Pullabrook Wood, which was blessed during the Beating the Bounds ceremony.

The culmination of events in 2000 was the Millennium Fayre in which the village centre was closed off and taken back in time with displays portraying Lustleigh through history from the Middle Ages, the coming of the age of steam, the World Wars up to the present day. A street market, thatched alehouse, street entertainers, period musicians, old agricultural machinery, vintage cars and a Town Crier, all helped to set the scene. A hog roast, strolling Shakespeare Players, Morris dancers from America, dramatic performances, children's parties and much more besides were rounded off with a floodlit barbecue.[34]

Lustleigh holds numerous events and fundraisers apart from the main ones. This photo is of a British Legion fete (date unknown) believed to have been held in Station Field near Brookfield.

8. Clubs & Societies

Committee of Lustleigh Unionist Association at the time of opening of the Lustleigh Unionist Club, November 16th 1911.
Back Row left to right, Jack Chudley, John Chudley (Orchard Farm), George Rice, Scott T Painter (Cleave Hotel)

Front Row left to right, Mr Edgcumbe, William Parr (Sanduck Farm), Ranulph Edward Glanville (The Crags), Edwin May (Rudge).

Lustleigh entertains

It is abundantly clear from the records that the people of Lustleigh have always had the ability and talent to entertain themselves. Early magazines and recollections are full of references to whist drives, concert parties and other entertainments.

As well as the Church Choir, villagers have had the opportunity to join a number of other choirs in the village over the years. In the late 1950s and 60s, there was the Women's Institute Choir, while more recently the Lustleigh Music Society Choir has performed a variety of music including "The Green Man" and "The Dartmoor Cantata" by local composer Will Carnell with words by Alexa Romanes.

The first reference to a drama group was when James Nutcombe Gould formed the Barn Owls in 1879. Over the next few years, its productions in the Rev. Frederic Ensor's barn at the Manor[35] included "The Merchant of Venice", "The Taming of the Shrew" and "Milky White". Between the wars, Arthur and Jack Gould were the leading lights of the Lustleigh Dramatic Society and in 1945, the Lustleigh Players was born, performing works by George Bernard Shaw, J.B. Priestley and Noel Coward under the leadership of Arthur Gould. Plays were performed in the Conservative Hall but were also taken to neighbouring towns and villages and occasionally the Hawkmoor Sanatorium.

During the 1960s, plays and pantomimes were performed under the banner of the Women's Institute until the present Lustleigh Drama Group was formed in 1973 since when it has put on pantomimes and plays as varied as "Wild Goose Chase", "She Stoops to Conquer" and "The Beggar's Opera". Since 1993 the Village Hall Committee has, with the support of Villages in Action, brought professional entertainment events to the village including dance, music and opera, children's shows, comedy and drama: among the highlights were performances of Welfare State International, Kneehigh, the Old Rope String Band, Rasa Theatre's "Curry Tales" and Black Voices.

CLOCKWISE FROM TOP: W.I. Drama Group; a Barn Owls programme; Lustleigh Drama Group panto with Tim Wakeham as the "dame"; the Barn Owls production "Phenomenon in a Smock Frock".

Village societies

Prior to the Parish Magazine's first publication in 1888, records of village organisations are rather thin on the ground. Possibly the longest established society that has been in continuous existence is the Garden Society, originally known as the Horticultural and Cottage Garden Society, which held its first show in 1887. It soon gained a reputation as 'quite the event of the year in the pretty little village',[36] drawing visitors from the surrounding district, with the benefit of the rail links, and 520 competitive entries being admitted.

The Archive Room.

Rather more recently, The Lustleigh Society was formed in 1978 to study and promote an interest in the history, archaeology and natural history of Lustleigh and the surrounding area; also to record the changing character

and traditions of the village and its neighbourhood. An important part of its work is the stewardship of documents, papers, photographs, recordings and digital records in the Community Archive. Collections include parish records and registers, parish magazines dating from the first issue in 1888, minutes of village organisations, postcards, paintings, books and other documents of historic interest. The Lustleigh Society also hosts a programme of lectures and visits on topics relevant to the aims of the Society.

The Lustleigh branch of the Women's Institute was formed in 1941 and its first speaker was the "Teign Valley Group authority on communal jam making" who insisted that the village needed to open a jam making centre[37] which it duly did in the Church House. Throughout the following two decades, the branch organised members' outings, exhibitions, demonstrations, children's parties and classes including upholstery and dressmaking. In the later years of the 20th century, the WI has been active on nationwide rural campaigns as well as tackling issues closer to home including local amenities and the future of local services such as the post office.

Outings

The coming of the railway opened up opportunities for villagers to go on group outings. In July 1890, the men of the church choir and ringers joined a party from Newton Abbot choir and went on an excursion by train to Hereford and Malvern to see 'a part of England unknown to them'. The first school excursion of children, teachers and parishioners went to Teignmouth by train on Saturday 1st September 1894.

The introduction of motor vehicles widened opportunities further. For example, charabanc trips were run by Mr. May and by the Osbornes at Brookfield

Bakery who organised excursions to Torquay, Paignton, Teignmouth, Dawlish etc.

"The school and Sunday school gave us an outing to the seaside each year... On the school trip we were taken by charabancs, a great adventure", recalls John Dray. "An interesting mode of transport was provided for the mothers. A Mr George Beer who owned the coal yard had a large lorry that he used for delivering the coal which he also used for animal transport by fixing slatted wooded sides and back. Come outing day, a small body complete with seats was bolted to the flat bed, and hey presto, it became a small coach."[38]

Village Hall

Since it first opened in 1911, the village hall has been the centre for many village activities. Initially known as the Constitutional Hall, and later the Conservative Hall, it was taken over in 1976 by the Parish Council and was completely rebuilt and extended in 2005; it is run by a dedicated committee of volunteers.

The village hall has been regularly used for meetings, classes, badminton, as well as plays, pantomimes and concerts. In the 1940s, it hosted a series of fancy dress balls and at one time there was an annual village children's party at Christmas. The British Legion held its annual dance there and it was also the venue for a smoking concert in 1942 for the local Home Guard and other local defence members.

Since the formation of the Home Guard, the hall has uniquely housed a rifle range and is home to the Lustleigh Home Guard Rifle Club, formed in 1944 originally to occupy local villagers as they came home from war.

The Lustleigh Rifle Club 1969 and two of their badges.

Sport

Records indicate that cricket was well established in Lustleigh by 1888 at which time the team played on a pitch adjacent to the Cleave Hotel (possibly the one still in use today) while the choir boys played cricket every Saturday in one of the fields at the Rectory. The present Lustleigh Cricket Club wasn't founded until 1938, at which point it considered moving to one of the fields belonging to Kelly Farm, but the decision was taken to remain at the ground, known as Lower Woodpark Meadow, and its location certainly attracts praise from various quarters. Peter O'Toole, who visited with his Lazarusians club, said in a 2007 Observer article, that it was his favourite ground of all those at which he had played across the world.

There are a few references to football being played in Lustleigh: it appears to have been a sporadic pastime, but at one time formed the joint Lustleigh Cricket and Football Club. In 1924, it changed its name to the Lustleigh Sports Club and took the decision to enlarge its activities with the laying down of a lawn tennis court and a bowling green immediately, "to have its eye upon all sorts of games" and to open its membership to both sexes. The following year, a club captain was appointed covering Cricket, Bowls and Tennis suggesting that football, once again, had fallen by the wayside: this was likely due to lack of support considering reports in other years of forfeited matches due to insufficient players.

Lustleigh has also had a darts team at various stages, sometimes organised under the auspices of the British Legion and on other occasions representing the Cleave Hotel, such as in 1941 when it won a tournament in aid of Moreton Cottage Hospital and successfully defended its title the following year.

Rangers and Guides outside the Village Hall.

Scouts and Guides

Lustleigh was very quick to respond to the call of Robert Baden-Powell, founder of the Scout Movement at the beginning of the 20th century and was among the first wave of groups to be formed around the country: the 1st Lustleigh Scouts being started by Captain Edwards and led by him for a number of years. It was a thriving unit for a very long time until being suspended before a revival in 2009 with 28 youngsters from the village and surrounding area forming Cub, Scouts and Explorer sections; unfortunately, due to lack of volunteer support, it closed once again in 2017. Alongside the Scouts, during the 20th century, there was also the 1st Lustleigh Guides, Rangers and Brownies who, like their male counterparts, regularly staged entertainment for the village including plays and folk dancing.

Rangers and Guides at Hound Tor, 1920.

Not a drop to drink

Teetotalism was becoming a strong movement in the village by the beginning of the 20th century. During one evening in April 1903, while the Lustleigh Total Abstinence Society were active in the Baptist Chapel, a meeting was taking place in the Board Schoolroom of the Church of England Temperance Society: at the end of proceedings, it was agreed to form a local branch of the Rechabites. Thus, the following month, "The Cleave Tent" came into being and quickly became a very active movement, even forming a 'juvenile tent' later that year.

This was a time of huge growth for the Rechabite nationwide movement with some 300 branches and 20,000 members being added annually. The Order particularly thanked the influence and support of the Lustleigh parish rector, Henry Tudor, who endorsed the "need for Temperance work in the village, not only among the working classes, but those who moved in higher stations in life. As the Vicar of the Parish, he had many opportunities of seeing the evils of the drink".[39]

As well as its mission to spread its temperance message, the Rechabites also functioned as a friendly society providing sickness benefits and life assurance to its members and regularly held fund raising events including an annual fête. They were not, however, the only organisation in the village with a similar function, there also being the Lustleigh Rational Sick and Burial Society and the two bodies almost came to blows one year. For many years, 'the Rationals' had a church parade on Whit-Sunday followed by a fête on Whit-Monday, but they decided against such activity in 1908 at which point the Rachabites stepped in; fearing they would annex the occasion permanently, the Rationals quickly announced their fête and a dispute ensued which the Rector tried to settle in vain.[40]

The Lustleigh Rechabites outside the Church House.

THIS PAGE, CLOCKWISE FROM TOP LEFT: Young Farmers' drama production; Lustleigh Girls club perform Rumpelstiltskin; Local hunt in the village centre, Easter 1929.

TOP:
Football Club, c.1927;

BOTTOM: Lustleigh Cricket Club early 1980s
Back row from left: Malcolm Northmore, Roger Olver, Irene Wright, Courtney Wright, Mick Dray, Derek Wills, Len Harvey, John de Sallis, Tony Perring, Doug Germon, Helen Wills, Mike Jacobs.
Middle row from left: Bob Barge, Phil Drewett, Richard Hughes, Mike Wright, Brian Edwards, Judy Barge
Front row from left: Shaun Wright, Tim Wakeham, Dave Neil, Steve Germon, Steve Wright.

Photograph courtesy of Dave Wills

9. Defence of the Realm

Wartime Lustleigh

Lustleigh people have always been willing to play their part in defence of King and Country. In both World Wars, many young Lustleigh men joined and fought in the armed services - some did not return. Those too young, too old or unfit joined the Defence Force Volunteers - later known as the Home Guard.

The Dray Brothers on leave together at Higher Combe in 1943 left to right, Ronald (Glider Pilot Rgmt), John (Northamptonshire Regmt), George (Royal Artillery).

Lustleigh Home Guard.

The women made their contributions too. During World War I, sphagnum moss was collected from the bogs on Dartmoor; there were weekly meetings to clean it and send it off for making dressings for wounds, thanks to its antiseptic properties. In February 1919, the Parish Magazine reported that "it has been found of the greatest use in the hospitals, and much in demand. Lustleigh moss has gone to many parts of England and abroad." The ladies of Lustleigh also helped at the Bovey Tracey Supply Depot making bandages for soldiers and sailors.[41]

The children, too, assisted in the collection of the sphagnum moss as well as foxglove leaves for medical purposes, in blackberry picking to aid the jam making and in collecting waste paper which was sent off to Cardiff as a further element in the war effort.

Homes were provided for evacuees during both

Mr and Mrs Van der Poorten, refugees from Belgium who lived at Elmfield.

Evacuees Annie, Joyce and George Cotton.

wars. Between 1914 and 1916, three families of Belgian refugees came to the village; during World War II, evacuee children swelled numbers in the school to a maximum of 140 in 1940. Iris Gould[42] remembers an evacuee family staying with them but they insisted on going back after only four days because they couldn't stand "the 'orrible 'ills and the 'ellish 'ush."

There was astonishment when a bomb fell on the railway line at Caseley; and further surprise, as Mrs. Ashton remembers, "when the first Yanks came into Lustleigh to shop, they thought they were Germans because of their helmets and called out the Home Guard."

There was rationing and some hardship — even after the War. Many families were grateful for the generosity of others as in March 1950 when sixteen old people in Lustleigh were given food parcels donated by the Canadian Red Cross. The end of World War II was celebrated with a bonfire on the Cleave (much as they had marked the Treaty of Versailles ending hostilities in 1919) and blanks were fired in the air.

Boer War

The two World Wars were not, of course, the only overseas battles that touched the village of Lustleigh. The wars in Africa, for example, at the end of the 19th century were supported by both deeds and action.

At the start of the Second Boer War in 1899, a 'Patriotic Concert' was held in the Church House, attended by over 200 and raising £13 12s 9d (£13.64) for the Association for Wives and Children of Soldiers and Sailors. A year later, the war was to claim the life of 19-year-old Charles Arthur Hamilton Baddeley who fell at the battle of Spion Kop, and whose sacrifice is remembered on a copper alms dish in the parish church. A few months later, came news of the relief of Mafeking and the school children of Lustleigh celebrated with a party in a field where the house called 'Brake' now stands.[43]

Supporting those fighting for our country, and their families, may even have been the driving force behind the formation of the Barn Owls amateur dramatic group: their first performance in 1879 of two one-act comedies, "A Phenomenon in a Smock Frock" and "Little Toddlekins", raised funds for the Isandula Relief Fund[44] which supported the widows and orphans of soldiers who had lost their lives fighting the Zulus in South Africa.

War memorial

The most enduring symbol of Lustleigh's part in the defence of the realm is, of course, the War Memorial at the foot of Mapstone Hill. Unveiled in 1925, it was the culmination of many years of debate which started as early as 1917 when a proposal was put forward to erect a War Shrine made of teak wood from HMS Britannia, surmounted by a cross of hammered copper from the same ship, but the idea didn't find support in the village.[45]

The main discussion for a permanent memorial began in 1919, initiated by Reverend Herbert Johnson who suggested a memorial chapel in the church. At a later public meeting, four ideas were considered and the one proffered by Cecil Torr was broadly adopted: "The names of those who fell should be put on a tablet in the church and a list of other names should be put up in the village, carved on either rock or some such suitable way".

The memorial tablet was unveiled in the church on 20th February 1921 by Colonel Bradford whose son's name was alphabetically first on the list. The larger memorial took somewhat longer to come to fruition, with fund raising not starting until a suitable site had been agreed, a piece of ground generously donated by Major-General W.J. Fawcett of St. Andrew's in Lustleigh: that was in 1924 with the unveiling ceremony taking place on April 11th the following year.

Initially, only 20 names of the 21 fallen were inscribed on the war memorial (even fewer on the church tablet but space here doesn't permit speculation as to reasons why). It wasn't until 1926, following representations by Mr Vanstone, headmaster of Lustleigh School, and Mr Horrell, a co-committee

member of the British Legion's Lustleigh branch, that the final name of H.E. Smith was added. It is interesting to note that the memorial actually remembers all those who fought, not just the fallen, courtesy of a hidden chamber beneath the granite base in which was placed a memorial roll of honour, compiled by Revd. Johnson, containing brief notes on 102 men and one woman who served in the Great War.

Members of the Lustleigh Branch of the British Legion pose for a photograph having received the deeds to the land on which the war memorial was to be built.

British Legion

It is probably fair to say that the British Legion was the driving force behind the construction of the War Memorial; moreover, it was claimed, at the time at least, "to be the only one in England, so far as can be ascertained, that has been erected entirely under the auspices of a local branch of the British Legion".[46]

The exact date of the formation of the Lustleigh branch is difficult to pinpoint as its early records were lost. Nationally, the British Legion (BL) was founded in 1921 when four organisations of ex-Servicemen were brought together. Certainly, there was a Lustleigh Post of the Comrades of the Great War (one of the four bodies preceding the BL) in 1921 and the following summer, an annual fête was held by the Lustleigh Comrades of the British Legion. It is likely, then, that the Lustleigh branch of the British Legion came into being somewhere between these two dates.

Colonel A.S. Dunlop, President of the Lustleigh branch of the BL, both designed the memorial and supervised its construction while other members of the Legion collected the necessary funds. At the unveiling ceremony, members of the Legion's Lustleigh branch also provided the guard of honour.

The unveiling of the War Memorial by General Sir Alexander J. Godley, K.C.B., K.C.M.G., on Saturday 11th April 1925.

In 2014, the Lustleigh Bellringers marked a hundred years since the outbreak of World War I by ringing a muffled peal of bells. On the 100th anniversary of the death of every man listed on the War Memorial, a muffled peal was rung. The Lustleigh Society researched the lives of these men and on occasion met their relatives. On the 10th February 2017, members of The Bunclark family gathered in the church to remember George Bunclark who was killed in Salonika in 1917.

10. Education

Lustleigh Junior Class, February 1961.
This photo was kindly supplied by Allyson Hayes, daughter of then headmaster John Dalton.

There is very little evidence of a school in Lustleigh before the 19th century though there might well have been a private, or 'dame' school at some point. The only reference to have been found is a response to the Bishop of Exeter in 1764 enquiring about village facilities such as almshouses, hospitals and schools etc. "We have a school, my lord, but no public one. We have only a Church House wherein our Poor People live, but no Alms House". [47]

Old Vestry

The first public school was established in 1825 by the curate, Rev. William Davy, who instigated the building, by public subscription, of a school in the north-west corner of the churchyard. The indenture stated that it was for "the educating and instructing of the poor Children being Parishioners of the said Parish of Lustleigh in the Principles of the Established Church of England in reading and needlework … and in such other proper and useful learning."

The Rev. Wm. Davy, at the Age of 82.

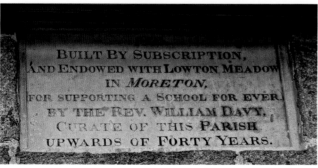

As a church school, the Rector taught Scripture and the teacher was responsible for teaching the 3Rs. Although Rev. Davy made an endowment to provide income for the school, it was insufficient to cover all of the costs and so a small fee had to be charged. In 1833, there were 24 children and, by the middle of the century, despite the building's small size, it was accommodating as many as 50 pupils.

TOP: Lustleigh schoolchildren and their teacher, 1927.

BOTTOM: School photograph from 1935.

Old school with church house in foreground.

ABOVE: The school bell.
LEFT: Long-serving headmaster, Mr Vanstone with his wife.

Old School

Following the 1870 Education Act, establishing the state system of education, the Lustleigh Board School was built in 1876 on land within a short distance of the old church school at a cost of nearly £1,200[48] to accommodate 75 children as well as a teacher's residence. At first, the school was divided into infants and senior (or upper) classes, with up to 40 pupils.

As time went on, numbers at the Board School increased and in 1892 it was enlarged for 125 children[49] and it was divided into three sections, with a junior section between the infants and seniors. One of the longest serving headmasters was Mr. Albert Vanstone who held that office for some 30 years, in which time 'he had started more than six hundred [pupils] on the journey of life'. There was a brief break in his teaching career when, during WW1, he served with the 6th Devon Regiment in India.

The school was inspected regularly, not only by the government but also unusually by the diocese and in 1891 the Diocesan Inspector reported: 'The school is classed as "good". This is very creditable to the Masters and Teachers… There is a marked improvement in the knowledge of the children since the last Inspection, the younger group are in very good order and reverent in tone, though too many remain silent. In the Upper group too the youngest children are not fully interested in the work, but the others answer very brightly, and many of them show good intelligence and produce very commendable results."

Children being children, they weren't all angels as some of the entries in the Punishment Book testify. On 18th October 1915, W. Moore received 'four stripes across the desk' for throwing a mushroom across the room; on the same day, four boys received 'one stroke on each hand' for chasing girls in the back office; in 1939, G. Dray was admonished for 'disobedience over changing shoes', although no punishment is recorded.[50]

There was great emphasis on good attendance. Prizes were given for full attendance, which was very difficult for those children who had to walk several miles to school from the outlying farms and in all weather. On the lighter side, there was always the annual school outing to look forward to, usually to Teignmouth. Also, the endowment left by Rev. Davy to fund the old school was now being used for prizes in the new school.

During WW1, children were asked to take a log each day to fuel the school stove as part of the war effort and they were encouraged to take an egg which would be their main meal along with a warm cup of cocoa. They also contributed to the war effort by collecting conkers, the 'flour' of which was used (in place of much needed grain) in the manufacture of cordite, a propellant used for firing weapons: on one day alone in 1917, the children collected a staggering 150kg of horse chestnuts.

During the Second World War, numbers at the school rose to about 140 with the arrival of evacuees. The Infant department was moved to the Church House close by, where the rest of the school joined them for lunch cooked on the premises. In 1948, with the raising of the school leaving age to 15, the Senior part of the school was closed and children aged over 11 went on to schools in Newton Abbot.

The school children were also, of course, kingpins in the May Day celebrations. Firstly, they would elect one of the girls to be May Queen and, on the day itself, four of the boys would carry a canopy of flowers above the Queen on her procession, while two others would carry her crown and sceptre. She would be followed by maids of honour and then the rest of the school children. Many practices were held at the school, with the procession and the dancing thoroughly rehearsed.

In 1963, the Western Morning News recorded the closing down of the village school due to falling numbers. Lustleigh children continued their State education at Bovey Tracey or Moretonhampstead Primary Schools until the age of 11, and then on to Newton Abbot or Ashburton for their secondary education.

Other schools and education

Unsurprisingly, throughout the decades, children from Lustleigh have also been sent away for a private education and occasionally, there has also been private schooling provided in the village. In 1868, it was reported that 'a movement is being made for establishing a middle-class school for boys in this most healthy and romantic neighbourhood'[51] with adverts claiming that 'the standard of education is that of the Oxford and Cambridge University Local Examinations'.[52] The school was possibly run by William Kirby, Curate[53] and School Master[54], living at Hillshayes[55] on Mapstone Hill. More recently, Church House was used as a small, privately run pre-school, lasting for some 13 years from 1989.

Also, in the distant past, there was an effort towards further education when a new twice-weekly Night School for men and boys over sixteen met for the first time in November 1880. It was 'fairly attended' and the first book was 'Uncle Tom's Cabin', although one is left wondering as to its success, considering that just two years later, we read that 'the ladies in Lustleigh propose opening a Night School'

A group of Lustleigh schoolchildren in the late 1930s.

in the hope that 'many young men and boys, who feel that they would like to go on learning and not to forget what they have already learnt, will come to it'.

Although all of the schools are gone, the village has the Lustleigh Orchard Pre-school and playgroup which offers "fun and learning from birth to 5 years of age". Meeting in the Village Hall, it gives pre-school children the opportunity to learn while having fun whether that's in the custom-built nature garden or doing 'simple science' play.

11. People of Note

Cecil Torr

In the 19th century Wreyland, which originally formed part of the Manor of Wreyland, was owned by the Torr family. The third generation, Cecil Torr, inherited the estate and whilst living in Yonder Wreyland wrote "*Small Talk at Wreyland*".

"Down here, when any of the older natives die, I hear people lamenting that so much local knowledge has died with them, and saying that they should have written things down. Fearing that this might soon be said of me, I got a book last Christmas - 1916 - and began to write things down."[56]

The three volumes draw a great deal from the diaries of his grandfather and father and are full of anecdotes and observations describing local people and customs; other local works include "*Wreyland Documents*" and "*A Survey of Wreyland*". Cecil Torr was, however a scholar, historian and writer of even greater significance publishing works on such varied subjects as ancient ships, Egyptian chronology and a theory of how Hannibal crossed the Alps.[57] He died in 1928 and is buried in the graveyard of the Unitarian Chapel at Moretonhampstead.

James Nutcombe Gould

One of the names most synonymous with drama in Lustleigh is Gould, and none moreso than James Nutcombe Gould. He had gained a passion for amateur dramatics while working in London at the Bank of England. He returned to Lustleigh where he grew up and in 1879 formed The Barn Owls which put on plays in the Rev. Ensor's barn at The Manor (previously the Rectory, now otherwise known as The Great Hall). Within a few years, however, he decided to return to London to take up the stage as a profession.

Although he joined a Shakespearian company in 1884 and found other roles subsequently, his first major professional appearance was in "*Brantinghame Hall*", a major break for him but unfortunately a major flop for its writer, W.S. Gilbert. During his career, he was regularly seen on West End stages and gained a reputation for comedic roles, apparently being the original Lord Darlington in Oscar Wilde's "*Lady Windermere's Fan*".[58] It was said that his forte was "aristocratic characters, and also genially cynical

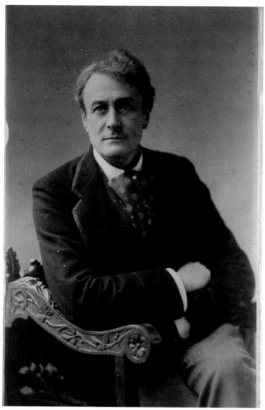

James Nutcombe Gould.

was, though, a revival of his fame, having originally enjoyed success in the 1930s. In between these times, he lived for a while in Lustleigh, at Underwood which he bought in the 1940s.

It is said that he took virtually no part in village life and just used the house for rest and recuperation. He had a housekeeper, a sweet widowed lady called Mrs. Coles, of whom he took advantage, getting her to carry his heavy case to the station, for example. After selling Underwood, he moved in with Mrs. Coles at Barn Cottage, Middle Wreyland, but soon tired of living in a small house and moved back to London.

Lord Hambledon

"Among great men who have been connected with Lustleigh, one of the greatest was Mr. W.H. Smith, the Leader of the House of Commons, whose death is deplored by the Queen, and by all sorts and conditions of men", so read an obituary in the parish magazine of November 1891.

It is unknown when his connection with the area started, but a year before his death, William Henry Smith, son of the founder of the WH Smith business, had purchased 5,000 acres of land from the Earl of Devon, an estate which included many ancient manors and almost 30 farms, probably including Sanduck. In 1903/4, his son William Frederick Danvers Smith bought Narramore and it

The Hon Frederick Smith
later 2nd Viscount Hambleden
1904

middle-aged gentlemen, and in the delineation of these he is without a rival".[59]

James Nutcombe Gould died in London in 1899 aged 50 and his body was brought back to Lustleigh for burial. That year, in his memory, his family erected the Gould Memorial Lantern in the churchyard where he is buried.

Stephan Grappelli

Those that know the name of Stephan Grappelli probably do so because of his popularity in the 1960s and 70s and maybe for his television appearances performing violin duets with Yehudi Menuhin. This

is thought that Fursdon also joined the estate at some point. One of W.F.D. Smith's most notable actions was the building of a Manor House just over the border in North Bovey which was converted into a hotel by Great Western Railway and is now known as Bovey Castle.

Like his father, W.F.D. Smith was a philanthropist and devoted as much of his time to good causes as to the family business. His contributions were both on a large scale, buying the land and contributing substantial funds to the building of King's College Hospital, and on a local scale with a cottage hospital in Moretonhampstead for "poor persons suffering from disease or accident and being resident in the parishes of Moretonhampstead, Chagford, Drewsteignton, Dunsford, Lustleigh, Manaton and Bridford".[60]

When Lord Hambledon, W.F.D. Smith, died in 1928, substantial death duties necessitated the selling of his Devon land holdings, with many properties being bought by sitting tenants.

Leopold Amery

The Amery family are said to have farmed on the borders of Dartmoor since 1515 and in the 19th century became one of the principal landowners in Lustleigh. Among the family's most famous sons was Leopold Stennett Amery who was born to Charles Frederick Amery who lived at Middle Combe, although Leopold was born at Gorakhpur, India while his father was serving with the Indian Forestry Commission.

His early career was in journalism and at the outbreak of the South African War he was *The Times* correspondent in Pretoria. He turned down editorships for both that newspaper and *The Observer*, choosing instead to concentrate on politics becoming a prominent Conservative minister.

Photograph courtesy of Churchill Archives Centre, The Papers of Leopold Amery, AMEL 10/1, Bassano Studio 1914

Among his many achievements, Leopold was a chief author of the Balfour Declaration of 1917 which called for "the establishment in Palestine of a national home for the Jewish people", in other words the creation of Israel. During other stages of his political career, in 1922 he was appointed First Lord to the Admiralty and from 1924 to 1929 he served as Secretary of State for the Colonies.

Leopold had two sons. One, Julian, lead a colourful and distinguished life as a wartime member of MI6, writer and politician and who was created a life peer in 1992 with the title Baron Amery of Lustleigh. The other, John, for acts of treason during WW2, was executed in 1945, hung by Albert Pierrepoint in Wandsworth Prison, the same year Leopold received the Companion of Honour.

Leopold was a keen mountaineer (and had three mountains named after him) and at his memorial service in Lustleigh in 1955, the Alpine Club was represented by Hugh Ruttledge (see below); his ashes were interred in the churchyard alongside several ancestors.[61]

Hugh Ruttledge

Hugh Ruttledge was a mountaineer of huge talent and by all accounts equal to Sir Edmund Hillary, the first man to reach the summit of Everest, but he was thwarted by a number of obstacles. Chief among the impediments

was that when Hugh Ruttledge made his two attempts on Everest, he was hampered by monsoons which made it "like trying to walk on tiles on a roof"[62] and almost impossible to function. Furthermore, during his first climb, which was in 1933, 20 years before Sir Edmund Hillary's triumph, access wasn't available from the Nepalese side and this therefore forced him to undertake a 300-mile trek to the northern side before even starting the ascent.

According to his daughter, his role was more to lead expeditions than to climb to the top; on that first expedition, he led a team of gentlemen explorers and native Tibetan sherpas, among them was Tenzing Norgay who famously accompanied Sir Edmund Hillary in 1953.

Sadly, when the Second World War came, the Tibet side of the mountain was closed off and prevented him from making any further attempts before his age forced him to hang up his crampons. About the same time, he moved to Lustleigh and lived with his family at Middle Combe.[63]

Carolyn Seaward

Evidently not a Devon Dumpling was Lustleigh's very own beauty queen, Carolyn Seaward, who lived at Long Close in the Village. After her first successes winning Miss England (and consequently second runner-up at Miss Universe) and Miss United Kingdom, Carolyn went on to be runner-up in the 1979 Miss World competition. A few years later, she appeared as a Bond Girl in the 1983 film *Octopussy*. For many years she ran the Lustleigh Horse Show and did the make-up for the Drama Group. Surely, though, her crowning glory was opening the Lustleigh Millennium Fayre in June 2000.

Martin Barre

Martin Barre was the lead guitarist with Jethro Tull for 43 years and is renowned for the 20th best guitar solo ever in the song Aqualung. Martin owned Higher Combe on Mapstone Hill in the 1970s and is rumoured to have created the two lakes with the intention of building a small-scale figure of eight steam railway around them. Martin tours world-wide with his own band and still lives in Devon.

12. Around the Village

Around Lustleigh parish can be found a fascinating collection of structures and features, many of which are uncommon, a few of which are unique, but all of which contribute to make our village the wonderous place that it is.

Bishop's Stone

One of the first landmarks to be encountered on entering the village is the Bishop's Stone, located on

Lustleigh, Bishop's Stone.

the right-hand side of the road shortly after crossing the old railway bridge. An octagonal block of granite, set in the hedge, it is said to have the arms of the See of Exeter on its front and the initials 'T.C.' on its back, but severe weathering makes these marks virtually impossible to see.

The most romantic theory is that it was named after Bishop Grandison, a 14th century Bishop of Exeter, who was once supposed to have dined upon the stone whilst passing through the village. An alternative theory is that it commemorates Thomas Comyn being instituted to the Rectory of Lustleigh by Bishop Cotton in 1607.

Datuidoc Stone

Another stone, and one of immense historic importance is the Datuidoc Stone which once lay sunk into the floor of the south porch of the church, just outside the church door, forming the outer threshold. In 1979, it was moved inside the church to avoid any further damage caused by years of wear. Dating from between 450 and 600AD, it bears the inscription DATUIDOC – CONHINOC – FILIVS[64] which means "The stone of Datuidoc, the son of Conhinoc". It was possibly erected in a pre-existing Christian graveyard, marking Datuidoc's original burial place. It is thought that both men were of local importance, perhaps members of the native land-controlling class who exercised authority in the west

Photograph by kind permission of © Chris Chapman

after Britain ceased to be a province of the western Roman Empire.[65]

Parson's Loaf

Half way up Mapstone Hill, on the right-hand side, is a huge granite rock from which the road takes its name. The rock is described as a 'panstone', that is to say it has a hollow on the top which collects water; nearby was a Saxon farm known as Maetta's farm. Thus, the rock was referred to as Maetta's panstone which, over the years, became shortened to Mapstone. It has been suggested that it was renamed in the Victorian era by those wishing to banish any possible connections with early druidic practices and called it The Parson's Brown Loaf, presumably in part due to its proximity to the old rectory.

Reproduced from a Harvey Barton & Son Postcard

Pound Cottages and Tudor Cross.

Tudor Cross

Another religious memorial can be found outside the church on the village green. Often mistaken for the village War Memorial, the Tudor Cross was erected "In pious memory of Henry Tudor, Rector of this Parish" who served Lustleigh between 1888 and 1904, following on from his father-in-law, the Rev. Frederic Ensor. An equally lasting memorial is the Parish Magazine which he founded during his first year in office.

Ash Houses

Around the parish can be found many examples of ash houses, a particularly local phenomenon with 85% of moorland ash houses found in the five neighbouring parishes of Lustleigh, Manaton, North Bovey, Moretonhampstead and Chagford.

As the name implies, these granite buildings

(usually circular) were used as a safe repository for hot wood ash from domestic fires to avoid sparks from embers setting light to thatched roofs. It was also a place where the ash could be kept dry before being used to supply potash to arable fields.

One explanation why these buildings are found on this part of Dartmoor compared, say, to the west is the preponderance of thatch on this side of the moor, whereas Cornish slate was the roofing material of choice in the west. Also, the drier climate here was more suitable for arable farming which would have benefited from the potash.[66]

© Roger Perry, reproduced by kind permission of Mrs Shirley Perry

Lower Hisley and Ash House.

In Lustleigh, the Ash House at Lower Hisley is said to be one of the best preserved, while others can be seen from the road at Sanduck and at Ellimore Farm; meanwhile, an example of the less common rectangular form can be found at Waye.

Hunter's Tor

Dartmoor has hundreds of hut circles and Lustleigh can claim several on the Cleave. They are traceable far back into the Bronze Age which began about 1900BC. At the north-western extremity of the Cleave range, at Hunter's

Tor, can be seen the remains of an Iron Age fort, dating from around 500BC. It is possible to identify ramparts and an artificial ditch and in the rough ground around it are the faint remains of a field system which appears to pre-date it.[67] Although it is referred to as a hill fort, it is likely to have been less of a defensive structure and more a place of security for the livestock and resources of a small group, possibly an extended family.[68]

Nutcracker Rock

Another granite landmark which could be found on the Cleave was a logan stone known as Nutcracker Rock. Located on Sharpitor, it got its name by being so finely balanced that little more than a finger could set it rocking with sufficient force to crack a nut. Unfortunately, in 1950 it was maliciously dislodged: by whom is unclear as several suspects were mentioned including the army and a local family, although a lady living at Nutcracker Cottage, Mrs. M.W. Cook, told a newspaper reporter that she "saw two men with crowbars... and they told me they were

going to push a boulder over... Had I known they intended to push over the Nutcracker, I would have done my best to stop them."[69]

The rock had landed in a precarious position and it was resolved to move it to a safer place. Eventually, the army volunteered to attempt to winch the rock back to its original position, but in the process it slipped and crashed down the Cleave splitting into several pieces. Its original site is, however, still known as Nutcracker.

Hisley Bridge

Another crossing of the River Bovey, and to be found in Hisley Woods, is a medieval packhorse bridge known as Hisley Bridge.

importance of the matter, described the walk along the path between the two villages, on which the bridge sits, as "one of the most beautiful in south Devon".

In 2007, DNP and Devon County Council declared the bridge unsafe and installed "an over-engineered monstrosity" made from steel and imported stone flown in by helicopter; it subsequently fenced off the clam bridge to prevent its use by the public. However, a local campaign, championed by the Lustleigh Society, led to its re-opening on 8th November 2016, securing the continued use of this river crossing which is thought to have been in place for over 140 years. It is now managed by Natural England and can be crossed "at your own risk".

Postcard F. Frith & Co

Clam Bridge

Along the Bovey Valley, in the vicinity of Foxworthy Mill, can be found a clam bridge, believed to be the last such structure still accessible on Dartmoor. Similar in construction to stone clapper bridges, it is made from two pieces of wood cut from the same tree and roughed to reduce slipperiness.[70] The nature of the material means that it needs periodic replacement, one such occasion being in 1896 when the parish magazine appealed for subscriptions, a suitable tree having already been donated by a Manaton resident. The article, highlighting the

Hammerslake Stile

A crossing of a different sort can be found at Hammerslake, one of Lustleigh's hamlets: it is an arched stone stile at the top of a flight of steps where a footpath leaves the lane and climbs towards the top of Lustleigh Cleave.[71]

Postcards F. Frith & Co

**CLOCKWISE
FROM TOP LEFT:**
Brookfield in 1917;
Cricket Club
Millenium stone;
Foxworthy Mill;
Village Centre,
early 20th century;
Pound Cottages.

Harton Chest on
Lustleigh Cleave.

Photograph © Jeremy Hepworth

TOP: Horsham Steps on the River Bovey near Foxworthy. BOTTOM: The Old Weir and Weir Pool at Hisley Bridge.

Postcards F. Frith & Co

Lustleigh

They folk that live in Plymouth
Their houses build in rows
With hard and chilly pavements
From Stonehouse to th' Hamoaze.
But those who dwell in Lustleigh
They plant 'em here an' there,
Just as the fancy takes 'em,
Wi' streamlets everywhere.

They folk that live to Plymouth
Their city desecrate
Wi' bold unlovely chimneys
An' staring roofs o' slate.
But up along to Lustleigh
The thatch is mauve an' brown,
An o'er the cottage windows
The eaves slope snugly down.

Postcard J. Welcht & Sons, Portsmouth

Why, down along to Plymouth
They boast about their Hoe,
But if you seek an orchard,
Backyards are all they know.
But gardens up to Lustleigh
Wander among the rocks
Wi' roses an' sweet-william
An' flaming hollyhocks.

They poor chaps down to Plymouth
I pity them for sure:
I'd rather bide at Lustleigh
Under the sheltering moor.
An' when my time be ended
An' the call comes to die,
Where graves are green at Lustleigh,
'Tis there that I would lie.

John Aston (1880-1937)
Dartmoor Lyrics and Other Poems,
Arthur Stockwell Ltd, London, 1929

References

[1] Worth, R.N., *"Tourist's Guide to South Devon"* 1886, p 76. London, Edward Stanford

[2] Mais, SPB, *"Glorious Devon"*, 3rd edition, 1934, p47. Paddington, Great Western Railway Company

[3] *Exeter and Plymouth Gazette*, 'Dartmoor Excursions', 2nd April 1900

[4] Betjeman, J., *"Devon Shell Guide"* 1936, pp29/30. London, Architectural Press.

[5] Crowdy, C., *"The Book of Lustleigh; Portrait of a Dartmoor Parish"*, 2001, p.17. Tiverton, Halsgrove

[6] Spelling variations include William le Prouz, William Prouze and William le Prouse

[7] Walter, N., "Quarrying in the Wrey Valley", *"In the Footsteps of the Victorians, Aspects of Change in the Wrey Valley and Surrounding Area, 1837-1901,"* p136. Exeter, The Lustleigh Society 2018

[8] Launched in Ireland in December 1931, the film was not on general release until 1932 (IMDb)

[9] *Great Western Railway Magazine*, "How the First British Train "Talkie" was made" (circa 1930)

[10] Worth, R.N., *"Tourist's Guide to South Devon"* 1886, p 76. London, Edward Stanford

[11] Cresswell, B.F., *"Dartmoor and its Surroundings"* 1909, p27. London, The Homeland Association

[12] *"A Pictorial and Descriptive Guide to Dartmoor"* (8th Edition) p50. London, Ward, Lock & Co. Ltd

[13] Torr, C., 1970. *"Small Talk at Wreyland"*, Combined edition, p56. Somerset, Adams & Dart

[14] Mais, SPB, *"Glorious Devon"*, 3rd edition, 1934, p47. Paddington, Great Western Railway Company

[15] Also sometimes recorded as Barne Court and Barn Court

[16] Wills, Mike, 2006. The WILLS Family of Lustleigh [online] Available at <http://website.lineone.net/~mike.wills/lustleighfarms.htm> [Accessed 18th December 2017]

[17] Higher Combe, Middle Combe and Lower Combe are all sometimes spelt Coombe

[18] An alternative spelling is Narramoor

[19] Taken from Peskett's unpublished *"A Brief History of Lustleigh"* circa 1969

[20] Other spellings included Boveycombe Cleve, Boviecombe Cleif and Boviecombe Cliffe

[21] For spelling variations see footnote 6

[22] Extract from *"A Talk on Old Lustleigh"* given by Mary Knight to Moretonhampstead WI, June 1973

[23] Crowdy, C., *"The Book of Lustleigh; Portrait of a Dartmoor Parish"*, 2001, p.144. Tiverton, Halsgrove

[24] Moore, T., *"The history of Devonshire"*, 1829. [online] Available at: <Google Books https://books.google.co.uk> [Accessed 19th December 2017]

[25] Polwhele, R. *"The History of Devonshire"*, Trewman & Son, 1797, Exeter,

[26] The Dartmoor Society, 2017. 20th Dartmoor Society Award 2017. Press Release, 23rd April 2017. Quote by Dr Tom Greeves

[27] *Western Times*, 26th September 1890

[28] *Western Times*, 'Lustleigh', 6th January 1928

[29] *Western Times*, 'Lustleigh', 8th September 1950

[30] *Western Times*, 'Royal Wedding of the Prince of Wales and Princess Alexandra', 17th March 1863

[31] *Exeter & Plymouth Gazette*, 'The Lustleigh Jubilee Celebrations', 24th June 1887

[32] *Western Times*, 'Lustleigh Railway Opening Celebration', 3rd August 1866

[33] Blackenstone is also referred to as Blackingstone

[34] Crowdy, C., "*The Book of Lustleigh; Portrait of a Dartmoor Parish*", 2001, p.154. Tiverton, Halsgrove

[35] 'Manor' was the name given to the original rectory on Mapstone Hill, even though it is unlikely to ever have served the purpose as the 'Manor House'

[36] *Exeter & Plymouth Gazette*, 'Lustleigh Flower Show', 3rd August 1897

[37] *Devon and Exeter Gazette*, 2nd May 1941

[38] Crowdy, C., "*The Book of Lustleigh; Portrait of a Dartmoor Parish*", 2001, p.142. Tiverton, Halsgrove

[39] *Western Times*, 2nd May 1904

[40] Torr, C., 1970. "*Small Talk at Wreyland*", Combined edition, pp58-9. Somerset, Adams & Dart

[41] *Western Times*, 28th March 1916

[42] "*Memories of World War II*", Lustleigh Community Archive

[43] Pellew, H. "*The Story of Waye in the Manor of Lustleigh*", 1986.

[44] *Western Times*, 9th May 1879

[45] *Western Times*, 15th May 1917.

[46] *Devon and Exeter Gazette*, 14th April 1925

[47] Revd. Johnson, H. *Some Account of "The Church House at Lustleigh*", 1925.

[48] *History, Gazetteer & Directory of Devon*, 1878-79, p530. Sheffield, William White. (Alternative document in Lustleigh Community Archive gives the cost as £200.)

[49] *Kelly's Directory of Devon & Cornwall 1893*, p320. London, Kelly & Co. Ltd.

[50] Extracts noted by Hilary Gould from documents held at the County Records Office

[51] *Western Times*, 3rd January 1868

[52] *Western Times*, 7th July 1868

[53] Henry W. Kirby was curate at Lustleigh 1870-1871

[54] 1871 England Wales & Scotland Census. Crown Copyright reproduced by courtesy of The National Archives, London. [online] Available at https://www.findmypast.co.uk [Accessed 2nd November 2017]

[55] Now known as Hill Hayes but previously known by various spellings including Hills Hay

[56] Torr, C., 1970. "*Small Talk at Wreyland*", Combined edition, p1. Somerset, Adams & Dart

[57] Buckman, D. [date unknown] "*Cecil Torr; a Devon author*", *Devon Life*

[58] "James Nutcombe Gould", Wikipedia [online] Available at https://en.wikipedia.org/wiki/James_Nutcombe_Gould [Accessed 22nd December 2017]

[59] Eglington, C., 1892. The Theatre [online] Available at <https://archive.org/stream/s4theatre20londuoft/s4theatre20londuoft_djvu.txt> [Accessed 19th August 2017]

[60] Simkins, M.A. & R.J.J., 1991. "Lord Hambledon and Moretonhampstead", *The Transactions of the Devonshire Association, vol 123, p175.*

[61] *Western Times*, 17th September 1955

[62] *Mid-Devon Advertiser*, 6th June 2003

[63] *Mid-Devon Advertiser*, 6th & 13th June 2003

[64] The inscription has also been interpreted as DATUIDOCI – CONHINOCI – FILIUS

[65] *Western Morning News* (date unknown)

[66] Perry, R., 1995. "Dartmoor's Enigmatic Ash-Houses", *Dartmoor Magazine*, p15.

[67] Taken from p546 of one of N. Pevsner's books on Devon (copy of extract held in Lustleigh Community Archive)

[68] *Hunter's Tor Hillfort, Lustleigh, Devon: an Earthwork Survey*. Ben Moore for English Heritage ISSN 1478-7008

[69] *Exeter & Plymouth Gazette*, 19th May 1950

[70] *Western Morning News*, 20th November 2008

[71] Harper, D., 2005. Wikimedia Commons [online] Available at https://commons.wikimedia.org/wiki/ File:Stile_at_Hammerslake,_Lustleigh_-_geograph. org.uk_-_127093.jpg [Accessed 18th December 2017]

NOTES:

1. All historical newspaper articles sourced from the British Newspaper Archive, available at www. britishnewspaperarchive.co.uk. (Articles accessed between August 2016 and December 2017)

2. In Chapter 4, *Manor and Farms*, extensive use has been made of the unpublished research *The Story of Waye in the Manor of Lustleigh* by Colonel H Pellew, who lived at Waye 1965 – 2004.

3. Other than those items referenced above, much of the material and documents used in researching for this book, and most of the photographs, are from the Lustleigh Community Archive.

Index